Behavior Description Interviewing

BEHAVIOR DESCRIPTION INTERVIEWING

New, Accurate, Cost-Effective

♦ **TOM JANZ, Ph.D.**
The University of Calgary, Alberta, Canada

♦ **LOWELL HELLERVIK, Ph.D.**
Personnel Decisions, Incorporated, Minneapolis

♦ **DAVID C. GILMORE, Ph.D.**
University of North Carolina at Charlotte

Allyn and Bacon, Inc.
Boston London Sydney Toronto

Library of Congress Cataloging-in-Publication Data

Janz, Tom.
  Behavior description interviewing.

  Includes bibliographies and index.
  1. Employment interviewing. 2. Organizational behavior. I. Hellervik, Lowell. II. Gilmore, David C. III. Title.
HF5549.5.I6J36 1986   658.3′1124   85-15059
ISBN 0-205-08597-0

Series editor: John Peters
Consulting editors: Kendrith M. Rowland, Gerald R. Ferris
Production coordinator: Helyn Pultz
Editorial-production services: Total Concept Associates
Cover coordinator: Linda K. Dickinson

Printed in the United States of America

10 9 8 7 6 5 4 3 2 1   89 88 87 86 85

Contents ◆

Preface ◆

We have written this book for people who want to make the best, most scientific hiring decisions within the structure of an interview. The people we have in mind come from many backgrounds. Some are new graduates of MBA programs, and others are seasoned alumni of the school of hard knocks. Some are engineers, scientists, and lawyers; others have backgrounds in logging, mining, farming, construction, or sales. These people have one thing in common. They will have to make decisions about whom to employ from a selection of applicants on the basis of a conversation we call the *selection interview*. This book should be required reading for people who want to interview as accurately and effectively as possible.

We have divided the book into four sections. Part I (Chapters 1 and 2) orients the reader and provides the background to behavior description (BD) interviewing. Part II (Chapters 3-6) introduces BD principles and provides the practitioner with the tools that are needed to begin BD interviewing. Part III (Chapters 7-9) builds the skills necessary for practicing BD interviewing, and Part IV (Chapter 10) completes the processes of applicant assessment and final decision making.

Part I, Chapter 1 describes the many advantages of behavior description interviewing. Chapter 2 then substantiates these advantages by referring to published literature and our on-the-job experiences.

In Part II, Chapter 3 carefully defines behavior description interviewing and explains its principles. Behavior description interviewing improves on traditional approaches by systematically probing what applicants have done in the past in situations similar to those they will face on the job. The concept that the best predictor of behavior in the future is behavior in the past is what this book is all about. Putting it into practice requires the skills and preparation provided in the remaining chapters.

Chapter 4 details how to analyze the job before interviewing applicants. Chapter 5 covers the legal side, clarifying the types of questions that are prohibited by equal opportunity guidelines. Chapter 6 takes the reader step by step through the process of writing interview pattern questions and shows how the job analysis leads to behavior description questions.

In Part III, Chapter 7 discusses how to open and structure the interview. It suggests proven ways to get the interview started on the right foot. Chapter 8 describes effective techniques for applying the interview pattern to obtain high-quality information. Chapter 9 focuses on special issues relevant to the recruiting interview.

In Part IV, Chapter 10 suggests an approach for sizing up applicants on the basis of interview notes and suggests three methods for reaching the interview decision, depending on job complexity.

Appendix A contains detailed BD patterns for sixteen jobs, from bank teller to systems analyst. The patterns are largely ready to use and suggest approaches to asking BD questions applicable to the entire range of jobs.

Appendix B outlines two different approaches that answer the bottom-line question: "Will BD interviewing pay off for me?" First, recent advances in costing the benefits and expenses of staffing programs appear as simple tables, and the reader can move step by step to an understanding of the potential return on investment BD interviewing can achieve. In addition, the appendix provides a verbal summary of BD advantages specific to various situations.

♦ ACKNOWLEDGMENTS

"The great chief is not the one who persuades most people to his point of view. It is rather the one in whose presence most find it easiest to arrive at truth" (Anonymous, appearing in "The legend of the Long House people," Dalton Camp, *The Canadian*, Nov. 1966).

As senior author, but by no means senior thinker, I list the names of my great chiefs:

Marvin Dunnette

John Campbell

Walter Borman

Lowell Hellervik

Joe Lischeron

Jack Peters

My thanks to all.

T. J.

PART I
Background ♦

CHAPTER ONE

Why Behavior Description Interviewing?

Behavior description (BD) interviewing directly benefits everyone involved with interviewing: the line manager, the human resource specialist, and the applicant. BD interviewing is *new*. It is not a minor facelift for traditional interviewing techniques; it differs substantially from them. BD interviewing accuracy exceeds traditional interviewing accuracy by three to seven times, and that improved accuracy makes BD interviewing highly cost-effective. Finally, cream-of-the-crop applicants prefer BD interviews and are more willing to accept jobs with organizations that use them. In short, BD interviewing rewards, challenges, and excites, but it also demands hard work. This chapter should convince you that the hard work will pay off handsomely.

The behavior description interview proceeds from a structured pattern of questions designed to probe the applicant's past behavior in specific situations, selected for their relevance to critical job events. Whereas traditional interviews obtain BD answers less than 5 percent of the time (Janz, 1982a), BD interviews assess each applicant against behaviorally defined job dimensions and obtain BD answers over 60 percent of the time. Hiring decisions flow directly from adding up the assessments.

Behavior description interviewing benefits all three actors on the interviewing stage: (1) the applicant, (2) the line manager, and (3) the human resource specialist.

♦ THE APPLICANT

Although each of these actors on the interviewing stage has a unique viewpoint and set of interests, they share some common interests. One of these common interests is to have job openings filled by the applicants who will make the greatest contribution to the organization once hired. We begin with the applicants because their interests seem so different from those of line managers and human resources specialists. First we will examine how accurate selection applies to an applicant's best interest. Then we will examine two related interests from the applicant's viewpoint.

The Applicant's Interest in Selection Accuracy

A devil's advocate might say that an applicant's only interest lies in being hired—that an applicant couldn't care less about his or her suitability for the job. We believe that most applicants are not so shortsighted. To examine this belief, consider the two kinds of selection errors and their impacts on the applicant.

False rejects
The first type of selection error falsely rejects an applicant who would actually fall in the high contributing group. This person should have been hired but was overlooked because of weakness in the selection method. The psychological costs to the applicant include the acute stress of disappointment added to the chronic stress that accompanies unemployment. The psychological costs of being rejected for employment exact a heavy toll, even for correctly rejected applicants. These costs intensify for applicants whose experience and skills would place them clearly among the top contributors but who just don't "shine" in poorly structured employment interviews.

False hires
What about the second type of selection error—the false hire? Being hired meets the applicant's immediate needs; the applicant is receiving positive feedback. Surely applicants need not fear the false hire. Unfortunately, the short-term gain often leads

to long-term pain. Placing an applicant in a job that is beyond his or her capacity is no favor. The likely outcome is humiliating task failures and eventual dismissal. Even worse, to solve the mess in one department, the unfortunate soul may be promoted out of the current misery into a position where that misery may be shared among undeserving subordinates. We have seen this happen in far too many cases.

In short, applicants have a clear interest in accurate selection decisions. As Chapter 2 notes, interviewers trained in patterned, behavior-based techniques produce much higher accuracy than is obtained by interviewers trained in standard techniques. Therefore, BD-trained interviewers make fewer of the kinds of mistakes that lead to unnecessary stress and failure for applicants.

The Applicant's Interest in
Interview Relevance

Selection tools can be highly accurate and at the same time seem largely irrelevant to the interviewee. Cognitive ability tests exemplify accurate but often irrelevant-appearing selection tools. Extensive research with thousands of people working in all kinds of jobs (Schmidt and Hunter, 1981) supports the accuracy of well-constructed cognitive ability tests for predicting on-the-job performance. Yet to the applicant who is taking the test, it all seems highly arbitrary and unrelated to eventual job performance.

Almost everyone can recall one or more interviews that completely overlooked the accomplishments and obvious weaknesses of the applicant. Sometimes the interviewer soars into a stratospheric discussion of philosophy that is never brought down to earth. Sometimes the interviewer wanders into a discussion of a sport or hobby he or she has in common with the applicant, and the interview into stories about "the Lakers' chances" or "the fish that got away." After the interview, the applicant realizes that the interviewer found out virtually nothing related to his or her potential contribution on the job. Applicants find nothing quite so disappointing as becoming "psyched up" to handle a probing interview, only to encounter irrelevant or vague questions.

So far, no one has accused the BD interview of being vague or irrelevant. In fact, reactions have been quite the opposite. In first glancing through the BD interview patterns (Appendix A), some interviewers who were experienced in traditional methods have commented: "I could never get away with asking those questions. They are far too personal and specific." Yet, as we document in Chapter 2, managers we have trained tell a different story. Top-quality applicants appreciate an interview that probes their specific accomplishments. One BD-trained manager queried all applicants who received offers from his company to find out why the offers were accepted or rejected. He reported that three top-notch applicants enthusiastically named the style of interview as the key reason for accepting the offer. According to this manager, the applicants reasoned that because the company demonstrated a high professional standard regarding how it hired new people, it was the kind of company they wanted to work for.

In a different setting, a company that recruited engineers shifted from traditional to BD interviews. The company noted that the proportion of offers accepted rose substantially following the implementation of BD interviewing. An informal followup drew applicant comments similar to the aforementioned reactions.

Thus, qualified applicants appreciate relevant, probing interviews that clearly size up their potential contribution to the organization. Top-notch applicants give BD interviews high marks for competence and relevance.

The Applicant's Interest in Interview Fairness

All applicants—but especially minority group applicants—find a common cause in the legal and moral requirements for selection fairness. The BD approach adopts the spirit of job relatedness, building it into every facet of the BD process. The BD questions themselves derive from a detailed behavioral analysis of the job, and the behaviorally defined job dimensions guide interview scoring. If a minority applicant is rejected after an interview that consisted of a rambling discussion of his college sports career, he is much more likely to perceive the interview decision as unfair than if the interview had involved discussions of his accomplishments and specific disappointments.

♦ THE LINE MANAGER

The line manager shares two key concerns with applicants, but from a different perspective. Line managers value their time and must account for the bottom-line performance of their subordinates. Accordingly, line managers share the applicants' interest in selection accuracy, but from their own perspective. Line managers also share an interest in applicants' perceptions of interview relevance. Managers want top-notch applicants to accept offers when they are extended. When chosen applicants accept most offers, it reduces the need to move down the list to less desirable applicants. We have already discussed the power of BD interviews to convince outstanding performers to accept offers. The remainder of this section expands on BD's organizational payoffs from the line manager's perspective.

The Line Manager's Interest in Selection Accuracy

Line managers are interested in accurate selection decisions for at least four reasons. First, if applicants unsuited to the job are hired, some of them are sure to leave of their own accord. These turnovers create more openings, which means that more money and time must be spent on recruiting, interviewing, and training. Worse yet, some unsuitable applicants will try to hang on, and a great deal of managerial time will have to be spent on (1) correcting avoidable problems, (2) endlessly repeating standard training exercises, and (3) documenting performance deficiencies. Add to these costs the opportunities lost by not having top-notch applicants contributing to the organization, and the bottom-line benefits of better selection stagger the imagination.

New advances in selection research into the selection utility formula allow us to measure and compare these costs. The selection utility formula relates the dollar savings for better selection programs to seven components of any selection program:

1. The number of openings
2. The number of applicants for each opening
3. The average tenure, in years

4. The accuracy of selection decisions on a scale from zero (no accuracy) to a maximum of 1.0 (perfect accuracy)—the correlation scale
5. The differences in annual dollar performance between performers in the top, middle, and bottom thirds
6. The dollars spent on recruitment
7. The dollars spent to process applicants once they are recruited

Some of these components may appear hard to pin down, but research has demonstrated sound measurement for all components (Hunter and Schmidt, 1983).

Appendix B explains how to cost out the potential dollar savings from implementing BD interviews in your organization. The appendix takes you step by step through the measurement of the seven components for your operation. It contains tables of the dollar savings per hire, per year of tenure from implementing BD interviewing (Janz, 1984). (It also includes notes that anticipate the expert reader's technical questions.) The following are two recently analyzed examples of such measurement.

A human resource (HR) specialist at a large local hospital anticipated making 490 hires for staff nurses over the next three years. Nurses stay about three years on average. We selected an accuracy improvement of 0.3 correlation units, since the hospital currently used unstructured interviews carried out by head nurses. The HR specialist selected $6,000 as the dollar spread of annual performance between top and bottom performers, and she projected five applicants for each opening. Given these numbers, the utility formula (see Appendix B) projected a total dollar benefit of $2,520 per hire × 490 hires × 3 years tenure = $3,704,400. How much would the savings cost? We base the additional cost of BD interviews on a time increase of 30 minutes per applicant; therefore, 0.5 hour × 2,450 applicants × $15 per hour = $18,375. We fix the costs of training line managers and human resources staff and developing the patterns at about $8,000. Thus, even though we used conservative estimates for the formula, the hospital clearly could save in excess of $3 million.

In another example, an oil company hires offshore drilling engineers to manage its platforms, and mistakes can be costly, since oil rigs bill out at $2 million per day. Management anticipated needing 11 senior offshore engineers over the next three years. They currently engaged "headhunters" to find the applicants. They found the tables in Appendix B inadequate to express the annual dollar spread between top and bottom performers, so we chose the $50,000 column. The company projected five applicants per opening. Offshore drilling engineers stay an average of five years. We set the accuracy improvement at 0.2 correlation units, because an engineer's professional reputation becomes widely known in this limited field. Total dollar benefits under these conservative assumptions work out to $14,000 per hire × 11 hires × 5 years tenure = $770,000 for an investment of about $10,000.

These two examples demonstrate the magnitude of the savings possible using behavior-based interviews. The size of the numbers seems incredible even to us. Yet if you step back and take a reasoned look, it makes good business sense. Put simply, most organizations have underinvested in the past. We all seek productivity, but investment, not faddish attentions, drives productivity. North America's high productivity in agriculture, for example, did not happen by accident. It happened through investment in developing appropriate genetic strains and efficient farm implements. Managing the productivity of human resources is no different. As a consequence of past sins, making modest investments now to apply BD technology can result in substantial dollar savings.

Summary

The line manager's interest in selection accuracy thus begins with the consequences of bad hires. Managers want to avoid wasting valuable time with poor performers who drag down the bottom-line showing for their unit, and the utility equation projects the cost savings made possible through BD interviewing.

At the risk of sounding overly dogmatic, we believe the bottom line speaks for itself. Whereas before we could only speak of the general value of hiring top-notch people, we now have two quantitative measurements: (1) how much it would cost to implement BD interviews and (2) how much it would cost *not* to do so. In the hospital example, the cost of implementing BD interviewing was about $27,000, but the long-run cost of staying with traditional, unstructured interviews was well over $3 million. The hospital management could choose not to invest $27,000 to implement BD interviewing today, but then it could *not* choose whether to spend the extra $3 million down the line. That $3 million would inevitably show up in unnecessary staffing levels, absenteeism, turnover, wasted supplies, and other results of ineffective nursing practice.

♦ THE HUMAN RESOURCE SPECIALIST

The human resource (HR) specialist shares the line manager's and the applicant's concern for accuracy and perceived relevance. Since the preceding two sections covered those shared interests, this section will concentrate on the dominant remaining concern—the HR specialist's interest in selection fairness and legality.

The impact of equal opportunity legislation and federal executive action has changed the face of selection practice in the United States. Canada and the European community lag behind, but they have many of the same concerns and practices. The Canadian province of Ontario, for example, recently adopted, almost intact, the list of proscribed interview questions circulated by the U.S. Equal Employment Opportunity Commission (EEOC). (Chapter 5 contains a list of questions to avoid.)

Although line managers retain ultimate responsibility for selection practices, the expertise for defending and developing defendable selection systems lies in the HR function. The legal definitions of disproportionate impact, job relatedness, test validation, and affirmative action are paramount, and position descriptions for HR management inevitably require a working knowledge of EEOC rulings and guidelines. We leave it to others to weigh the pros and cons of legal developments; this section relates them to selection interviewing and to BD interviewing in particular.

The enactment of Title VII, prohibiting discriminatory hiring practices, and the subsequent legal decisions, beginning with the *Griggs* v. *Duke* power case, radically altered how management thinks about the selection process. Because employment testing came under fire first, one reaction was to eliminate testing and stick to the unstructured interview. As Schmidt and Hunter (1981) pointed out, however, the costs of eliminating testing sometimes greatly exceeded the costs of defending a valid test. So far, we are unaware of court cases that set out preferred interview processes, although the EEOC does list questions that can lead to challenges to interview decisions (see Chapter 5). We believe that the interview is likely to come under increased legal scrutiny. Therefore, BD interviewing equips its practitioners to defend their decisions in the following ways.

First, following Bob Guion's (1976) advice, BD interviewers build a strong hypothesis that relates their interview questions to on-the-job performance. They build this strong hypothesis by first discovering the behaviors that differentiate effective and ineffective performers and then deriving interview questions that focus on critical job-related situations from the applicant's past.

Once the questions are asked and the applicant's responses are noted, BD interviewing requires that each applicant be assessed against the behavioral job dimensions. In this way, the rating process magnifies the direct relationship between job behavior and interview content.

We feel that the strong relationship between job behavior and interview content, magnified by the applicant assessment process, is a strong argument for the legal defensibility of properly conducted BD interviews. This can be illustrated by the following anecdote.

One of us trained the staff of a municipal parks and recreation division to interview students for summer staff jobs. The job types ranged from pool superintendents to life guards, camp counselors, and the like. Full-time staff members, who had developed BD interview patterns for each job, considered an increased ability to defend their selection decisions to be one of the positive outcomes of the BD program. Many more students applied for the summer positions than could be hired, and sometimes, when the son or daughter of a prominent civic figure was refused a job, the office received an angry phone call the next day. In the past, such calls had produced considerable stress and caution on management's part. With BD interviewing in place, however, the managers receiving these calls went to the file, read the notes, and found little difficulty in clearly explaining why a particular applicant was refused. They reported greater confidence in their decisions and satisfaction in being able to calm down irate "bigwigs" with the facts. Although this was not a court case, it does illustrate the improved defensibility of BD interview decisions.

♦ REFERENCES

Guion, R.M. 1976. Recruiting, selection, and job placement. In Marvin D. Dunnette (Ed.), *Handbook of industrial and organizational psychology*. Chicago: Rand McNally.

Hunter, J.E., and Schmidt, F.L. 1983. Quantifying the effects of psychological interventions on employee job performance and workforce productivity. *American Psychologist, 38,* 473–478.

Janz, J.T. 1984. Bottom line savings for behavior-based interviews. *International Journal of Management, 1,* 33–40.

Schmidt, F.L., and Hunter, J.E. 1981. Employment testing: Old theories and new research findings. *American Psychologist, 36,* 1128–1137. for the energy industry. *Journal of Canadian Petroleum Technology, 21,* 80–84.

Janz, J.T. 1984. Bottom line savings for behavior based interviews. *International Journal of Management, 1,* 33–40.

Schmidt, F.L., and Hunter, J.E. 1981. Employment testing: Old theories and new research findings. *American Psychologist, 36,* 1128–1137.

CHAPTER TWO

What We Know from Research and Experience

Many opinions on "how to interview" have appeared in print. Although this book also contains some of our opinions, it argues the merits of behavior description interviewing on the basis of evidence from research and experience. Even if your goal is simply to make better selection decisions, sooner or later someone will want to know what stands behind your new approach. Therefore, read on to be prepared.

The chapter is divided into two main parts. The first part reviews research on interviewing, including documentation of the deficiencies of the unstructured interview and discussion of five improvements to traditional interviewing—all of which are characteristic of behavior description interviewing. The five improvements are (1) structuring the interview, (2) defining job requirements, (3) basing questions on behavioral analysis, (4) taking notes, and (5) assessing applicants on job-related dimensions.

The second part describes five practical applications of behavior description interviewing. These descriptions add life to the message documented in the research and illustrate useful variations in the practical application of BD interviewing principles.

13

♦ RESEARCH ON BETTER INTERVIEWING

This section is not intended to be a comprehensive review of the interviewing literature, since several comprehensive reviews already exist (Arvey and Campion, 1982; Mayfield, 1964; Schmitt, 1976; Wagner, 1949; Webster, 1982). The accumulated evidence has documented the poor accuracy of traditional, unstructured interviews in predicting job performance, and recent research has probed the reasons for this failure. Webster (1982), for example, explores the topic in detail. The review here concentrates on research findings that support behavior description interviewing principles and procedures.

How Bad Is the Unstructured Interview?

Wagner (1949), going back to 1919, reported that none other than Alfred Binet, the inventor of intelligence testing, first tried interviews. He had three schoolteachers interview the same five children to assess their intelligence. When Binet asked the teachers whether they were confident of their assessments, they responded that they were. There was only one problem. They disagreed widely about the students' intelligence levels. Binet then abandoned the interview in favor of more rigorous testing methods.

Wagner (1949) also reported on three other early studies of the selection interview—Scott (1915), Scott, Bingham, and Whipple (1916), and Hollingsworth (1922)—which were similar to Binet's study but more sophisticated. Hollingsworth (1922) examined rankings given applicants for postings in the army. The same applicants were interviewed by several classification officers, but there was little agreement among ranks assigned by different classification officers. When several interviewers ranking the same man can't agree, it must be assumed that at least some of them err in judgment. Hollingsworth (1922) described one case in which an applicant was ranked first by one officer and fifty-seventh by another officer. Thus, this early research established the low validity of the unstructured selection interview.

Let's zoom ahead in time and put a number on the accuracy of the unstructured selection interview. Human resource specialists state the accuracy of any selection method on a correlation scale that ranges from -1.0 to 1.0. A value of zero means random or useless selection decisions; a value of 1.0 or -1.0 means that the hiring tool perfectly predicts eventual on-the-job performance.

To provide a frame of reference, Schmidt and Hunter (1981) reviewed hundreds of studies relating scores on cognitive ability tests to training or job performance. They reported that the tests ranged in accuracy from .26 for simple, routine jobs to the mid .50s for mentally demanding jobs.

Reviewing and combining all reported validation studies provides the best fix on the accuracy of a particular hiring tool. In a report of such an analysis at a conference on validity generalization, Ofsanko (1983) cited the best estimate of interview validity as .14. But what does this .14 rating mean? Certainly, 14 percent accuracy sounds pretty poor.

Look at it this way. If you could perfectly pick the very best applicants (the ones who would work out best once hired), selection accuracy would be 1.0. You would capture *all* of the human resource potential in the applicant pool. An accuracy rating of 0.14 means that you get only 14 percent of that potential. Its better than zero, but far below the .50 capture rate studies have demonstrated for behavior-based interviews. At the top end, even expensive, sophisticated, selection assessment centers lasting several days only raise accuracy to the .60s.

The following sections describe research that supports each of the major improvements that can be derived from applying the principles of behavior description interviewing.

Research on the Importance of Structure

Wonderlic (1942), another intelligence tester, advocated using a structured set of questions so that each applicant is taken over the same ground. McMurray (1947) reported support for "patterned interviews," as these structured interviews were called. In McMurray's study, scores from a patterned interview at one company correlated .68 with job performance ratings and .43 with length-of-service data. At a second company, interview ratings correlated .61 with length of service.

Somewhat later, Younge (1956) reported the findings of a patterned interview that was specifically designed to assess six performance topics. The median rank-order correlation between supervisor ratings of suitability and applicants' interview scores was .71. In a more recent study of structured interviews, Mayfield, Brown, and Hamstra (1980) used a "selection interview blueprint" to train personnel officers in the insurance industry. They concluded that interviewers can agree when they are making ratings about factual characteristics and that interview structure improves interview reliability. Four additional studies (reviewed later in the discussion of behavior-based question content) also support the advantages of an interview pattern. A study by Heneman, Schwab, Huett, and Ford (1975) did not support the advantages of interview structure. However, the study used videotapes of fake interviews, and the people playing the applicants were already employed. It is therefore difficult to tell how seriously the interviewers took their task in this study.

Thus, research findings generally have been in favor of increased interview structure, since structure often improves interview accuracy and validity. Covering the same performance topics with all applicants makes sense when the goal is a clear basis for applicant comparisons.

Research Supporting Clear Knowledge of Job Requirements

Would the same set of "all-purpose" questions do for all jobs, or should the interviewer be familiar with specific job requirements? Langdale and Weitz (1973) reported significantly higher interviewer agreement among interviewers who had been supplied with detailed job information. (Interviewers in the control group received only a job title.) Leonard (1974) also demonstrated that interviewers agreed better on topics that were relevant to the purpose of the interview.

Wiener and Schneiderman (1974) reported an elaborate study that considered the relevancy of favorable and unfavorable applicant characteristics. Half of the hypothetical applicants were evaluated by managers who had studied a complete job description. The rest of the applicants were evaluated by managers who had no job information. The researchers found that the managers who had studied the job description were less influenced by irrelevant facts that had been programmed into the hypothetical applicants.

In short, knowledge of specific job requirements enhances interview decision quality.

Behavior-Based Question Content

Given the findings that an interview pattern based on knowledge of job requirements helps interview accuracy, we can now consider research that suggests how the pattern questions should be formed.

In 1941, Dudycha reported a successful approach to predicting punctuality using the interview. He asked applicants what they would do in situations that called for punctual behavior. This was the first behavior-based approach to writing interview questions.

Maas (1965) moved the notion of behavior-based questions several steps forward. He began by having interviewers who were familiar with the job list traits of successful performers. Then the interviewers wrote behavioral examples of high, medium, and low performance on those traits. Finally, a separate set of managers sorted the examples into performance level, without knowing which level they were supposed to be. The behavior examples that managers sorted into the same levels intended by the interviewers who wrote them were retained, and the interviewers rated applicants' responses against these examples. Maas (1965) reported high interviewer agreement—.58 in one study and .69 in a second.

Latham, Saari, Purcell, and Campion (1980) refined the Maas procedure into what they called the situational interview. Instead of having interviewers merely list traits, they began with critical incidents of job performance—that is, stories that describe specific events that exemplify effective or ineffective job performance. Interview pattern writers turned the critical incidents into questions by asking applicants how they "would perform" in the described circumstances. The situational interview designers also prepared benchmark answers to guide interviewers when rating applicant responses to the behavior-based questions. Latham et al. (1980) reported interviewer reliability for the situational interview of .71 and .67 in two studies. Also in support of the validity of the situational interview, interview scores correlated .46 and .30 with supervisory performance ratings.

Janz (1982) reported a direct comparison of traditional unstructured interviews with behavior description interviews. Eight senior business students received behavior description interview training and eight other students were trained on standard interview process skills. A total of fifteen teaching assistants were interviewed four times, twice by interviewers trained in behavior description interviewing and twice by interviewers trained in standard techniques. All interviewers had a maximum of 30 minutes to gather information and predict the teaching ratings the teaching assistants would receive at the end of the term. Later in the term, the actual teaching ratings were gathered and compared with the ratings predicted by the interviewers.

We determined whether the BD-trained interviewers actually asked different kinds of questions and obtained more BD answers by taping all 60 interviews, but because of technical and operator difficulties, we obtained only 45 complete tapes. These 45 tapes were scrutinized, and each question was categorized as credentials, experiences, opinions, or behavior descriptions. We also grouped each applicant's answers into the same four categories. Thus, we directly compared the types of questions and answers used by traditional versus BD-trained interviewers. Table 2.1 details the comparison.

Clearly, the training produced substantial differences in the types of questions and answers used by the traditional and BD interviewers. Thus, we have established that BD interviews are different—but are they more accurate? We found that the standard interviewers demonstrated better agreement (.71 vs. .46), but the behavior description interviewers more accurately predicted subsequent teaching ratings (.54 vs. .08)—the "bottom-line" criterion for teaching assistant (TA) performance.

An in-depth look at the data suggested why the standard interviewers agreed with each other, but on the wrong TAs. Some TAs in the business faculty were downtowners, who dressed and sounded like businesspeople. They were older and had job experi-

Table 2.1
Information Type Percentages for Traditional Versus Behavior Description Interviews

Information Type	Traditional Interview	Behavior Description Interview
Credentials	15	4
Experiences	32	40
Opinions	48	23
Behavior descriptions	5	33

ence. Other TAs were graduate students, who didn't look much like businesspeople. The downtown TAs were also more aloof and less responsive to student concerns, whereas the graduate student TAs could identify better with the students and were actually better TAs. Thus, the standard interviewers liked the downtowners and disliked the graduates. They could agree on this. The problem was that they picked the wrong TAs to get high teaching ratings.

The behavior description interviewers had a tougher time agreeing. (They assessed the TAs on five behavioral dimensions of TA performance, and their disagreements fell on either side of the TA's eventual student ratings.) However, the behavior description interviewers more accurately predicted eventual TA student ratings by several times.

We report this substantial difference in accuracy to alert you to the size of the possible increase in accuracy if you apply the procedures in this book rigorously. Instead of looking forward to retaining only the 14 percent of the human resource pool potential, you can retain as much as 55 percent. (As mentioned earlier, the tables in appendix B will help you tally up the dollar benefits.)

To round out the evidence for behavior-based question content, Latham and Saari (1983) reported another concurrent validation study of the situational interview for clerical workers. They found that supervisor ratings and peer ratings of job performance correlated .39 and .42 with situational interview scores.

So far, the evidence in support of behavior-based questions is positive and strong. However, more studies are needed to support these initial findings and to prompt further improvements to the behavior-based methods of pattern formation.

Research on Taking Notes

The Life Insurance Management Research Association (LIMRA) conducted several studies on the interview, one of which investigated the impact of note taking on content retention (LIMRA, 1974). In this study, insurance managers listened to a 20-question taped interview with a prospective agent. They all had note-taking materials available. After they had heard the tape, the managers were asked to recall what they had heard. Some managers recalled all the answers; others recalled only five. It was found that those with the high scores had taken notes.

A study by Schuh (1978) also examined the effects of note taking and interruption on interviewer recall. The researcher showed company interviewers one of two different videotapes and told half the interviewers to take notes and the other half not to do so. One videotape contained a short interruption at the beginning. The highest retention of content from the tape occurred for interviewers who took notes and did not see the interrupted videotape. In short, the evidence weighs in on the side of taking notes before assessing applicants.

Research on Applicant Assessment

Several studies have addressed the final step in the behavior description process—how and when to assess the applicant. Two key questions dominate the discussion: (1) whether the interviewer should size up the applicant during the interview or after it is over and (2) whether the interviewer should make a simple accept/reject decision or an assessment of the applicant on key job-related performance topics.

Younge (1956) was critical of the interviewing practice reported at the time. He particularly criticized unstructured interviewing for having poorly defined objectives, for not knowing what to measure, and for using poor measures of job criteria. His solution included assessing the applicant following the interview on carefully defined performance dimensions. As noted earlier, the median correlation between supervisor job performance ratings and interview assessments was .71 in his study.

Asher (1970) started out to examine the effects of appearance on reliability and validity, but a secondary manipulation in that study bears more directly on the discussion here. In one research condition, applicants rated videotaped interviews and made three-point ratings on each of several questions. In a second condition, a single rating was made following the interview. In all conditions, interviewer agreement was higher for a combination of the three-point ratings than it was for the single rating made at the end of the interview.

The research findings on behavior-based interviewing reported by Latham et al. (1980), Janz (1982), and Latham and Saari (1983) all support methods in which the interviewers gather information during the interview and make assessments on specific performance topics following a review of interview notes.

Summary

Research has provided evidence that the following improvements should be made to the traditional, unstructured interview. First, the interviewer should be working from a pattern of questions that take all applicants through roughly the same performance topics. Second, the topics should be closely job-related. Third, the job-related topics should focus on job performance features that have been found to indicate the difference between effective and ineffective performers. Fourth, the interviewer should assess the applicant on the basis of a set of notes. Finally, the interviewer should assess the applicant on job-related performance topics following the completion of the interview.

Later chapters provide the step-by-step detail for achieving the high levels of selection decision accuracy reported for patterned, behavior-based interviews. The research reported here is useful only if it helps convince you to take those steps.

♦ EXPERIENCES WITH BEHAVIOR DESCRIPTION INTERVIEWING

If this book were meant to be digested by completely logical beings, the cold light of reason shining over research would convince all skeptics and motivate immediate adoption of improved interview methods. Fortunately, however, we are human, and nothing interests and communicates to us as well as practical experiences. Therefore, we have chosen five success stories to share with you.

Crossfield Laboratories: Regional Soils Sales Representative

The president of Crossfield Laboratories, Jim Mullis, Sr., approached one of us after reading a story about BD interviewing in his local newspaper's business pages. Crossfield Laboratories chemically analyzes soils and animal feed samples, and Jim needed a regional sales representative for its first expansion territory.

Jim Mullis, Sr., a chemical engineer by training and an entrepreneur at heart, had been owner-manager of several chemical technology firms. As he put it, "I made some good and poor hires, but I'm smart enough to know how costly the poor ones are." He worried, therefore, about the risks that accompany seat-of-the-pants interviewing.

We began a systematic BD interviewing program by interviewing Jim and his sales manager—Jim Junior—to develop examples of effective and ineffective sales performance. Next, we interviewed current customers of Crossfield Labs to gather more stories. Most of these interviews were conducted by phone. Then, armed with a pile of critical incidents describing effective and ineffective sales rep performance, we constructed a job pattern. We showed it to Jim Senior and Jim Junior, and they made a few additional suggestions for the operational pattern.

With the pattern completed, we began training Jim Senior and Jim Junior on using it effectively. Our manual for BD workshops guided them through two days of training exercises, and videotapes of effective behavior description interviews and practice interviewing brought them up to speed. They worked hard and always completed their reading of the sections of the manual before we began working on them. Jim Senior was an old pro and worked smoothly with the Behavior Description questions. Although Jim Junior was naturally less confident, by the end of training he, too, moved smoothly and persistently through the pattern.

Advertisements for the sales rep opening were placed in local farm community papers. Jim Senior and Jim Junior worked out an effective division of labor for the actual interviews: Jim Junior directed the questions while Jim Senior took notes. Jim Senior also stepped in and followed up in tricky spots when an applicant seemed to be sliding away from a behavior description question. After receiving 56 resumes, prescreening of the applications produced a short list of five qualified applicants, and interviews were arranged in the new territory's capital city. All interviews were taped so that we could evaluate the applicants independent of how Jim Senior and Jim Junior sized them up.

On returning to Crossfield, both Jims confidently announced that they had found a top performer, but they held off on making an offer until we could review the tapes and complete an independent assessment.

When we listened to the taped interviews, the payoff for our careful training appeared repeatedly. When an applicant started to slip away on a particular question, Jim Senior slid in smoothly to get the behavior description answer. When we compared our assessments to the assessments made by both Jims, we found that we had selected the same applicant, and we had agreed strongly on scoring of the others.

The chosen applicant, Les, was hired and sold over $200,000 in soils testing in his first two months. He also closed over 80 percent of his cold calls. When the sales season was over, Les remarked to Jim Senior: "Now I can get on with the real job, servicing my customers and providing support."

Clearly, we had reached an effective decision, but Jim Senior told us that he would have hired a different applicant if he hadn't used behavior description interviewing. Les had the least sales and soils analysis experience of the five applicants, and Jim Senior had felt that Les did not come across positively in the interview. We then reanalyzed Les's interview tape and noted that Les had evaded the behavior description questions because he was simply not familiar with that type of question. When the Jims pinned him down, however, he gave excellent answers. Other applicants sounded more eager and willing to blow their own horns, yet when it came down to how they behaved in job-related circumstances, Les stood out from the rest.

Until a bit later, we weren't sure that Jim Senior was right when he said that he would not have chosen Les if he had used a traditional interview. In preparing a demonstration for a convention presentation, we took excerpts from the taped interviews of three of the Crossfield applicants—one from Les's interview, the others from interviews with rejected applicants. We played the tapes to a roomful of psychologists at the convention, and only one chose Les as the applicant who had been hired and who had sold $200,000 in soils testing. It so happened that the one psychologist to correctly identify the high-performing applicant was Gary Latham, mentioned earlier as the developer of the situational interview. We also played the tapes to a class of 50 business students. Not one chose Les.

Jim Senior had been right. Les had evaded the behavior description answers and he had not played up his own responsibility for accomplishing tasks, whereas other applicants had tried to paint rosy pictures of their skills. Without the behavior description pattern and the skills to use it properly, interviewers can easily fall prey to applicants who are skilled at creating a good impression. Consequently, organizations often miss out on the talents of high performers who come across less favorably in interviews. The same reasoning accounted for the aforementioned results reported by Janz (1982).

To cap the story off, all the additional work created by Les's sales success meant that Crossfield needed more lab staff. Jim Senior said, "From now on, we won't hire anyone without a Behavior Description pattern in place." Thus, the success with the first pattern led to our writing a second one for lab assistant. (Both patterns appear in Appendix A.)

B.C. Hydro: Computer Programmer, Systems Analyst

Sherman Kwan, manager of corporate information systems for B.C. Hydro, a large provincial power utility, had attended an early behavior description interviewing workshop. Sherman appreciated the usefulness of cognitive ability tests for identifying good performers for the jobs of programmer and analyst, but the personnel department took a long time to get back with test results. He needed an accurate method for identifying quality computer staff that short-circuited the delay for test scoring, since the long waits for test results often meant that good applicants accepted positions elsewhere.

Therefore, in January 1982, four Hydro supervisors who were trained in BD interviewing developed a common pattern for interviewing 32 graduates of the local institute of technology. Twelve students were hired and, according to Sherman, they have all proved to be excellent employees. What's more, the successful hires were heard to comment favorably on Hydro's interviews as the most in-depth interviews of all employers visiting the institute.

First Chicago Bank: Credit Management Trainees

First Chicago Bank asked Personnel Decisions, Inc., to develop a system of sequential BD interviews for the position of credit management trainee. The applicants were largely new MBAs, who were interviewed during a day-long, on-site visit following on-campus screening. We developed an interview pattern using the BD methods outlined in this book.

As Crossfield had done, the bank management worked out a useful division of labor. Since each applicant met with several managers, the managers decided ahead of time which performance dimensions they would emphasize. This allowed for greater depth when the pieces were put together after the applicant left. At least two managers focused on each of the behavioral job dimensions.

Bank management has reported the success of the program on two fronts. First, they noticed a substantially higher rate of acceptance for offers; more of the really top-notch applicants accepted bank offers than before. Second, the training department at the bank, which is completely separate from the managers who perform selection decisions, reported that the first BD-selected group was "the brightest crop of people we have seen in a while."

Bailey and Rose: Systems Analysts, Computer Programmers

Bailey and Rose is an international computer software firm specializing in sophisticated systems development. Ken Harrap, a manager charged with recruiting staff abroad, had attended an early BD interviewing workshop. Immediately following the workshop, Ken faced 100 interviews in Britain on a mission to search out top talent for the firm. On his return, Ken told the following story.

Ken was satisfied with his improved ability to size up the advantages and drawbacks presented by applicants, but something else excited him more. In debriefing all the analysts who accepted offers with Bailey and Rose, he observed that several of the really top-notch applicants cited the thoroughness and professional competence of the interview as a prime factor in their decision to take a job with the firm. According to Ken, the applicants had reasoned that because Bailey and Rose demonstrated such high professional hiring standards, it was the kind of firm they wanted to join. Ken added one personal illustration to make his point.

One high-quality applicant whose reputation had preceded

him had wanted a job in Vancouver. However, although the BD interview had strongly impressed this applicant, by his own report, Bailey and Rose had no openings in Vancouver. Ken informed him that the firm wanted to hire him and asked him to check back later. The applicant did call back later, informing Bailey and Rose that he now had an offer from a firm in Vancouver but that he would prefer a job with Bailey and Rose. Ken still had no openings for this applicant's special skills in Vancouver, but he did have one in Ottawa, on the other side of the country. The analyst accepted the job in Ottawa.

Honeywell: Staffing a Residential Products Division

A residential products division of Honeywell asked Personnel Decisions, Inc., to design and install a BD interviewing system. Once again, the company expressed satisfaction with the improved selection quality, but reported it with a twist.

Applicants who had refused offers were sent a questionnaire, and a bonus was awarded to them if they responded. The questionnaire probed the applicants' reasons for refusing the offers and included spaces for open-ended responses. The Honeywell managers were impressed that many of the applicants who had rejected offers commented favorably on the quality and thoroughness of their BD interviews.

♦ SELF-TEST

1. On a scale of 0 to 1.0, how accurate are traditional, unstructured selection interviews for predicting job performance?

2. Define five improvements to interviewing that are supported by research evidence.

3. Considering all the studies of patterned, behavior-based interviews, how accurate are such interviews in predicting job behavior?

4. What is an unintended consequence of thorough, patterned interviews that helps reduce interviewing costs while attracting the "cream of the crop"?

♦ REFERENCES

Arvey, R.D., and Campion, J.E. 1982. The employment interview: A summary and review of recent research. *Personnel Psychology, 35,* 281–322.

Asher, J.J. 1970. How the applicant's appearance affects the reliability and validity of the interview. *Educational and Psychological Measurement, 30,* 687–695.

Dudycha, C.J. 1941. A suggestion for interviewing for dependability based on student behavior. *Journal of Applied Psychology, 25,* 227–231.

Heneman, H.G., III; Schwab, D.P.; Huett, D.L.; and Ford, J.J. 1975. Interviewer validity as a function of interview structure, biographical data, and interview order. *Journal of Applied Psychology, 60,* 748–753.

Hollingsworth, H.L. 1922. *Judging human character.* New York: Appleton.

Janz, J.T. 1982. Initial comparisons of patterned behavior description interviews vs. unstructured interviews. *Journal of Applied Psychology, 67,* 577–580.

Langdale, J.A., and Weitz, J. 1973. Estimating the influence of job information on interviewer agreement. *Journal of Applied Psychology, 57,* 23–27.

Latham, G.P., and Saari, L.M. 1982. *The situational interview: Examining what people say versus what they do versus what they have done.* Unpublished manuscript, University of Washington, Seattle.

Latham, G.P.; Saari, L.M.; Purcell, E.D.; and Campion, M.A. 1980. The situational interview. *Journal of Applied Psychology, 65,* 422–427.

Leonard, R.L. 1974. Relevance and reliability of the interview. *Psychological Reports, 32,* 1331–1334.

Life Insurance Marketing and Research Association. 1974. *Face to face.* Hartford, CT: LIMRA.

Maas, J.B. 1965. Patterned scaled expectation interview. *Journal of Applied Psychology, 49,* 431–433.

Mayfield, E.E. 1964. The selection interview: A re-evaluation of published research. *Personnel Psychology, 17,* 239–260.

Mayfield, E.E.; Brown, S.H.; and Hamstra, B.W. 1980. Selection interviewing in the life insurance industry: An update of research and practice. *Personnel Psychology, 33,* 725–740.

McMurray, R.N. 1947. Validating the patterned interview. *Personnel, 23,* 2–11.

Ofsanko, F. 1983. Validity generalization: Report of a conference. *Industrial Psychologist, 20,* 34–36.

Schmidt, F.L., and Hunter, J.E. 1981. Employment testing: Old theories and new research findings. *American Psychologist, 36,* 1128–1137.

Schmitt, N. 1976. Social and situational determinants of interview decisions: Implications for the employment interview. *Personnel Psychology, 29,* 79-101.

Schuh, A.J. 1980. Effects of early interruption and note taking on listening accuracy and decision making in the interview. *Bulletin of the Psychonomic Society, 13,* 263-264.

Scott, W.D. 1915. Scientific selection of salesmen. *Advertising and Selling Magazine,* October.

Scott, W.D.; Bingham, W.V.; and Whipple, G.M. 1916. Scientific selection of a salesman. *Salesmenship, 4,* 106-108.

Wagner, R. 1949. The employment interview: A critical summary. *Personnel Psychology, 2,* 17-46.

Webster, E.C. 1982. *The employment interview: A social judgment process.* Schomberg, Ontario: S.I.P. Publications.

Wiener, Y., and Schneiderman, M.I. 1974. Use of job information as a criterion in employment decisions of interviewers. *Journal of Applied Psychology, 59,* 699-704.

Wonderlic, E.C. 1942. Improving interviewing technique. *Personnel, 18,* 232-238.

Younge, K.A. 1956. The value of the interview: An orientation and a pilot study. *Journal of Applied Psychology, 40,* 25-31.

PART II

Principles and Procedures ♦

CHAPTER THREE

The Principles of Behavior Description Interviewing

♦ AN INTERVIEWING PARADOX

A major paradox exists in the field of selection interviewing as practiced by untrained interviewers: Although interviewers almost unanimously agree that the best predictor of future behavior is past behavior, they do not act as though they believe it when they interview. We assert that they spend the large majority of their time gathering information that must be considered "low-yield" information (in the context of the strengths of the interview process as a contributor to making selection decisions). We use the term *low-yield* to imply that almost any kind of information can be of some use, but it is not a very good way to use the precious time available in the interview process.

What is the problem? Why do interviewers not live up to their principles by seeking past behavior information that would relate to their decision about the candidate for the future? The first answer, we believe, is that interviewers do not know the difference between high-quality information and low-quality/low-yield information. The second answer is that interviewers don't know *how* to ask questions that will elicit high-quality information.

31

♦ SELECTION PRINCIPLES

We have found that solutions to the problems implied in both of these answers can be addressed through an interview information taxonomy—a categorizing system that defines various types of information emerging from interviews, thus conceptually clarifying those types for interviewers. In addition, a good definition of each category can include questions designed to elicit information of that type, thus demonstrating the "how" of obtaining that information.

Before moving into the taxonomy itself, however, we feel a need to refine the oft-quoted principles of personnel prediction. As stated earlier, most interviewers will agree very quickly to the popular principle that the best predictor of future behavior is past behavior. However, we think the principle can be refined nicely, without too much added complexity, as follows: The best predictor of future behavior/performance is past behavior/performance *in similar circumstances.*

The phrase *in similar circumstances* has powerful implications for interviewers. First, it directs us toward the circumstances *in the future* into which we intend to place the candidate. This calls for some form of careful job analysis. Second, it directs us toward the circumstances *in the past* that are *as similar as possible* to those into which we wish to put the person in the future. Most of us learned in introductory psychology courses that no two events are ever exactly alike. Therefore, it is impossible to find totally similar and perfectly congruent circumstances. The best we can hope for is a set of circumstances in the person's past that are highly similar to those into which we wish to put the person in the future. At all times, then, the interviewer must be intellectually alert to reasonable extrapolation from the job analysis findings to the individual's background and back again. *It's the part of the activity that makes interviewing challenging and fun.*

This facet of our principle also answers a common type of question: "What can you ask high school graduates who are applying for a file clerk job? They have no experience." That is the remark of a person who does not truly believe the principle! There *are* certain points in a person's life when prediction is more difficult because the gap in similarity between past circumstances and future circumstances is much wider than normal. However, the width of this gap does not invalidate the principle—

it just makes prediction harder and increases the challenge for the interviewer to perform the extrapolation tasks.

This principle, sometimes called the *behavior consistency principle,* is good—the best available—but it is not perfect, because people grow, change, deteriorate. Thus, two corollaries to this principle take change into account:

> *Corollary 1.* The more recent the past behavior, the greater its predictive power.

> *Corollary 2.* The more longstanding the behavior, the greater its predictive power.

Corollary 1 neither denies nor overvalues behavior from earlier stages of a person's career or life, but it does encourage the interviewer to focus most heavily on the most recent past behavior in similar circumstances. Corollary 2 encourages the interviewer to seek more than one sample of past behavior in similar circumstances. It does not permit overreaction to a single example in either a positive or negative direction.

♦ AN INTERVIEW INFORMATION TAXONOMY

A taxonomy is simply a way of classifying something—in this case, information that emerges in an interview. Table 3.1 shows the interview information taxonomy in a nutshell.

Table 3.1
Interview Information Taxonomy

   I. Biographical Facts, Credentials, and Achievements
  II. Technical Knowledge
 III. Experience/Activity Descriptions
 IV. Self-Evaluative Information
   A. Likes and Dislikes
   B. Strengths and Weaknesses
   C. Statements of Goals/Attitudes/Philosophy
   D. Hypothetical/Speculative Statements
  V. Behavior Descriptions

For each category of information, let's consider questions that tap each type of data. Keep in mind that some of the questions here are listed strictly for illustrative purposes, without regard to whether or not they are "legal" or "appropriate" according to equal employment regulations and guidelines. Job relevance is the key criterion for determining the appropriateness/legality of questions, so some questions that are illegal or inappropriate for one position may be perfectly acceptable for another.

Biographical Facts, Credentials, and Achievements

There are some data that can be verified by someone, somewhere. Theoretically, at least, there should be no argument about these data, because they can be substantiated and are not subject to opinion or judgment. For example, the following questions could be asked to determine biographical facts:

- What is your age?
- What is your marital status?
- How many children do you have?
- Where do you live?
- How many brothers and sisters do you have?

to elicit credentials:

- What is your degree?
- What is your major?
- Do you have a driver's license?
- What was your grade point average?
- List your professional articles.

and to find out about achievements:

- What honors did you achieve?
- What special recognition did you achieve?
- What awards or commendations did you receive?
- What size budget did you manage?
- What was your sales quota?
- By how much did you exceed your sales quota?

Much of this information could be documented on a piece of paper by the candidate and therefore could be considered "low-yield" information for the purposes of a flexible information-gathering tool such as an interview. However, since a single form is often used for all positions within a company, interviewers are expected to ferret out any special achievements, credentials, and so forth, that are related to a specific job. The key, however, is relevance. How relevant are the questions and answers for the particular position? Many of these questions are the kinds that are considered to be illegal or inappropriate today because they are not related to job performance, they have an unfair impact on minority groups and women, and they are simply not relevant to the job. In general, achievements and credentials are most important in making a *screening* decision, not a selection decision. Achievements and credentials are important information for evaluating a person's motivations, but the interview probably should be directed toward gathering more subtle information.

Technical Knowledge

Sometimes interviewers confuse technical knowledge with credentials. Most interviewers tend to assume adequate technical knowledge, given the right kind of job experience or academic training. However, some interviewers are fanatics about evaluating technical knowledge in the interview. They will often have a number of favorite in-depth questions that are designed to tap the right kind of knowledge in their area. This is much like a college professor constructing a paper-and-pencil achievement test.

Although such tests can be developed to yield good information about a person's technical knowledge, the problem is more difficult than laymen tend to believe. The problem is to make test items (questions) at the right difficulty level, such that a person without the right kind of technical knowledge cannot answer them and a person with the right technical knowledge can. Thus, the questions cannot be either too hard or too easy.

A simple caricatured example will illustrate these points:

Interviewer: Do you know how to type?

Interviewee: Yes.

This question does *not* satisfy the requirement for a technical knowledge question, since it does not assure the interviewer that the interviewee has the technical knowledge of "how to type." The respondent could be "faking it," and the interviewer would not be able to discriminate between those who know how to type and those who do not. Further questions may help illuminate but may not satisfy the requirements for technical knowledge questions:

Interviewer: How many words per minute can you type?

Interviewee: One hundred and eleven words per minute.

This question was *too easy,* because most people know that good typists type somewhere around 50, 70, 90 words per minute. Only if the candidate responded with a ludicrous number would the interviewer know that the candidate did not know how to type. Thus, the question is unlikely to separate successfully those who know from those who don't know how to type.
　　Another possibility is as follows:

Interviewer: Name the bottom row of keys on the typewriter keyboard.

Interviewee: (Pause...no response)

or

Interviewer: How do you set the margin on an IBM Selectric?

Interviewee: I don't know. I have never typed on an IBM Selectric.

Both of these questions were *too hard* for different reasons, and they conceivably eliminate many people who are really very efficient typists. In the first case, typing is such an automatic skill that it is difficult for many typists to recall exactly where keys are located. In the second case, the person's lack of exposure to a specific typewriter could lead the interviewer to eliminate a candidate who is, in fact, an effective typist.
　　Granted, these are caricatured examples, but those who are asking technical knowledge questions in interviews need to be

aware of the difficulty in constructing such questions with the right degree of relevancy and toughness.

Experience/Activity Descriptions

This kind of information is simply the kinds of activities or experience the person has had in the past. These are the most common kinds of questions in initial employment interviews. Here are some sample questions:

♦ What were your duties in that job?
♦ Tell me about your responsibilities in the last position.
♦ What did you study in your nuclear physics course?
♦ What did you do for your senior project?

Work experience is, of course, important to know. Other things being equal, we would generally prefer to have someone who knows our industry, products, services, and so forth, as specifically as possible. On the other hand, this kind of information leads to some of the major errors in interviewing and selection. Too many interviewers get tripped up by the "experience equals excellence" fallacy. *They assume that a candidate who has done something has done it well.* Unfortunately, when interviewers talk about experience/activity descriptions with others, they are well aware that experience does not mean excellence; however, in actual interviewing behavior, a neutral observer would conclude that the interviewer was satisfied that a narration of a given experience by the interviewee *must* mean that the person was, indeed, quite good at that experience. Interviewers seem to have the intellectual recognition that experience does not equal excellence, but they don't tend to behave that way in the interview. In fact, the applicant may be on the job market *because* of ineffective performance in that experience. Even if the candidate performed effectively in that activity or experience, effectiveness in it may have involved different behaviors from those required for effectiveness on the new job.

Self-Evaluative Information

These are the kinds of data that a candidate provides about himself or herself, and they are filtered through the interpretive lens of the person. These are also the kinds of data for which external observers can often provide an individual with "an objective view," because the person is "too close to it" in one way or another.

Likes and dislikes
These are the kinds of questions that get at the candidate's feelings of what he or she found enjoyable/motivating or not enjoyable/punishing. Typical questions are as follows:

- ♦ What did you like best about the job?
- ♦ What did you like least about the job?
- ♦ What was your favorite activity there?

Likes and dislikes are considered self-evaluative in the sense that the person has very limited exposure to the whole range of companies, schools, instructors, bosses, and so forth, that might be referred to in such questions. It is conceivable, for example, that a person who enjoyed supervisory work at a children's summer camp might despise supervising in a heavy manufacturing factory. A person's statement of enjoyment of supervision, then, is more a reflection of the person's evaluation of himself or herself in a particular environment than something truly objective.

Too often, interviewers fall prey to the assumption that what people like, they also do well, and what people dislike, they do poorly. Unfortunately, the reality of that is not at all clear. There is probably a low positive correlation between "liking" something and "performing well" at it. However, the correlation is low enough so that one cannot assume that "likes equals excellence."

Strengths and weaknesses
This is the core of self-evaluative data. Most interviewers ask strengths and weaknesses questions, and assume a position of enormous skepticism about the responses—probably justifiably so.

Goals, attitudes, philosophy
This is the area where most manager-interviewers like to spend their time. Typical questions are as follows:

- Where do you want to be five years from now?
- Why do you want this job?
- Why did you apply to this company?
- What is your marketing philosophy?
- How do you feel about working for a demanding boss?
- How do you feel about working overtime?

And a million others. The responses to these kinds of questions can be useful, but they are likely to be vastly overrated. We do not always perform in accordance with our goals, nor do we consistently perform in concert with our attitudes or philosophies. We all know of people who talk a good game about supervision but behave quite differently on the job. This is a common phenomenon so interviewers must be highly skeptical about responses to such questions as reliable indicators of future behavior.

The responses to these kinds of questions are also the most likely to be intellectualized. Candidates who are highly verbal have an enormous advantage in this area. Also, those who have the ability to articulate specific goals (real, or concocted for the purpose of the interview) have an enormous advantage. Verbalizations of attitudes that are similar to those of the interviewer are extremely potent in forming the interviewer's judgment—too often erroneously.

Hypothetical/speculative statements
These are the kinds of questions and responses that are referenced not in past behavior but in hypothetical behavior. The questions are like the following:

- What would you do if an employee called in sick three Mondays in a row?
- What would you do if you were working for a manager/ executive who refused to set priorities for you?
- What would you do if an employee told you she or he was not willing to work overtime when required?

Like the "goals, attitudes, philosophy" category, this category also gives an advantage to those who are intellectually alert and verbal. One highly esteemed interviewing researcher advocates questions of the "what would you do if" variety. His carefully conceived interview patterns include possible responses for each question, with different weights assigned to each response. His approach thus approximates an oral test. We believe that this approach is most appropriate when the job content requires one best way of behaving; but the "oral test" approach is less effective where a variety of styles may work. In addition, oral test questions tell you whether the applicant knows how he or she *should* handle the situation, but not whether she or he is likely to handle it that way. It's better to look for similar behavior in past similar circumstances—how the person handled it the last time.

Behavior Description Information

These data are those that are as close as possible to the actual behavior that went on in a given situation—the nitty-gritty detail of "What did he say?" "What did you say?" "What did he say then?", and the like. Here are examples of these types of questions:

- ♦ Tell me about your best accomplishment in your last job. Start with where you got the idea; describe how you planned to carry it out, how you executed your plan, and how you dealt with the major obstacle you had to overcome. (The same questions can, of course, be asked about a variety of situations. Also, the question can be reversed to ask about the biggest disappointment and the obstacle the person was unable to overcome.)
- ♦ Tell me about yesterday. I'm interested in all the nitty-gritty detail of the day, from the time you hit the office until the time you went home.

Also, to tap the area being investigated:

- ♦ Tell me about the *last* time you faced the situation of an employee who wasn't performing. What was the situation, how did you deal with it, what did you say, what did the employee say, and so forth?
- ♦ Tell me about the *most emotional* confrontation you had with your boss in that job.
- ♦ Tell me about the *least effective* performer you have ever supervised.
- ♦ Tell me about the *hardest* you worked in that part-time job.

  ♦ Tell me about the *best* public contact performance you had in the hamburger stand.
  ♦ Tell me about the co-worker you liked *least*.

The responses to these kinds of questions, especially when followed up with further behavior description questions, will also yield close approximations to what the person did, indeed, does in the given situation. It is almost as though the interviewer is watching that person perform in the workplace. Consequently, the responses are relatively raw and unfiltered data. Since they are raw data, they permit the interviewer to perform the analysis independent of what the person thinks of himself or herself in that situation. Consequently, asking behavior description questions is an excellent tool for cracking through the dynamics of situations in which the candidate is attempting to project an overly favorable impression.

Notice that superlative adjectives—those that indicate the greatest extent or degree of something (most, last, least, toughest, worst, etc.)—are the key to effective behavior description questions. There are a number of compelling reasons why the superlative adjective is an important component of a high-quality behavior description question. First, the question tends to stimulate specific events in the minds of the interviewee, and it is then easier for the interviewee to respond. Second, the interviewer knows something about where the incident fits on the scale of all similar incidents. That is, if it is the "most" of a particular quality, it is the most that can be expected if the interviewer believes in the principle that the best predictor of future behavior is past behavior in similar circumstances. The same is true if it is the "least" of a quality. This gives a more accurate reading of the event than simply asking: "Give me an example." Third, a superlative adjective is remarkably freeing on the respondent. It implies: "Of course, you have had one of these. I (as the interviewer) expect you to have had an incident like this and, furthermore, do not think you are a jerk because you have had such an incident." It's easy to see the compelling power of such questions by asking yourself which of the following approaches to a content area would get a better response from you:

1. Have you had any trouble with a co-worker? Give me an example.
2. Tell me about the co-worker you get along with *least,*

including how the problem developed and the *highest* tension interaction the two of you had.

All of the different types of questions discussed here have their place in the selection process. However, in our view, the "best" interview questions are behavior description questions. They are the only ones that yield detailed information about how the candidate behaved in the past in circumstances as similar as possible to those that the individual will be in in the future (if the interviewer has done his or her job analysis well and is creative at asking behavior description questions). Furthermore, such information is less likely to be distorted or misinterpreted than the information generated by other types of questioning. It does require more training to acquire the knack of asking behavior description questions and probing to gain the information one needs to make quality judgments. Interview formats are less tidy, since the questions tend to be longer, more involved, and more specific, as well as requiring more probing. However, as we will see later, formats can be developed quite successfully. The disadvantages, in our judgment, are rather minor in comparison to the significant gains from pursuing behavior description data in the selection interview.

♦ SELF-TEST

1. What is the behavior consistency principle as it is commonly expressed?

2. What is the foremost problem with traditional interviews?

3. What are two refinements or corollaries to the behavior consistency principle?

4. Define and give examples of three types of "low-yield" questions interviewers often use. What are their drawbacks?

5. What is the format for asking behavior description questions? Illustrate with an example.

CHAPTER FOUR

Job Analysis: Gathering the Pieces for the Pattern

The set of behavior description questions designed for a specific job, which is called a pattern, guides the interview over common performance topics, but not necessarily the same questions, for each applicant. The process of developing an effective interview pattern begins with a behavioral job analysis.

A behavioral job analysis is much more than a job description. Whereas a job description states the duties, responsibilities, minimum occupational standards, remuneration, and benefits of a particular job, a behavioral job analysis identifies what effective versus ineffective workers *do* in specific job-related situations. Even the most complete job description does not specify situations from an applicant's past that can predict future behavior on the job. The critical incident technique—a method of job analysis introduced in the 1950s by John Flanagan (1954)— leads to good BD interview questions that do identify such predictive situations.

♦ THE CRITICAL INCIDENT TECHNIQUE

Toward the end of World War II, in an attempt to improve the performance of bomber and tank crews, military/industrial psychologists interviewed field commanders, officers, and soldiers. In reviewing the mountain of material these interviewers had gathered, Flanagan (1954) observed that when an officer or crew member was asked to describe what he thought made for an "effective tank crew," he responded with a list of traits, or vague descriptions, such as courage, leadership, know-how, and the like. If the interviewer asked for an example of what he was getting at, the officer or soldier described a specific incident that was an example of effective or ineffective tank crew performance. These "stories" about specific tank crew behavior helped the interviewers identify performance problems and improve tank crew effectiveness. Flanagan coined the term *critical incidents* for such stories of real events that describe specific effective or ineffective job performance.

Critical incidents are valuable for several reasons. First, they are *data,* not opinions. Whereas opinions are limited by the insight and intelligence of one person, the data provided in a carefully gathered critical incident depend only on the memory and observational skills of the person. All the forces in play can be described, even if they are not understood by the person who is describing the incident.

Second, incidents can be gathered from several types of sources—for example, both up and down the hierarchy in an organization and from customers or inspectors. Then the incidents from different sources can be compared or simply pooled. Such pooling of incidents from several sources gives a wider perspective that is less subject to the biases inherent in opinions.

Third, critical incidents lead directly to behavior description questions for applicants with related job experience. For applicants without directly related job experience, the interview pattern writer must creatively develop other situations that are similar to those described in a job-related incident but are drawn from general situations that applicants are likely to have experienced.

Chapter 6 details the mechanics of forming pattern questions, and Appendix A contains many interview patterns, including questions for applicants with both direct and indirect job-related experiences. This chapter provides detailed "how-to" suggestions for carrying out behavioral job analyses.

Even if you are implementing behavior description interviewing for a job in the same general category as one analyzed in Appendix A, we suggest that you do a behavioral job analysis, for several reasons. First, the legal and moral defensibility of the interview pattern will be increased if you check the completeness of the pattern. Second, you can add the flavor of your organization to various words and phrases contained in the pattern. Of course, it is not necessary to interview as many sources or gather as many incidents as you would if you were starting from scratch.

A third reason for seeking local incidents goes beyond adding a question or rephrasing to fit local terms. It strikes at two key principles mentioned in the book *In Search of Excellence* (Peters and Waterman, 1982): (1) productivity through people and (2) closeness to the customer. By actively and equally listening to input from executives, supervisors, and incumbents, an organization demonstrates its concern for its people. Also, by gathering incidents from customers, the organization promotes a practice noted as characteristic of excellent companies—that is, involving customers in all aspects of innovation and growth.

You may think that you already know what makes the difference between an effective and ineffective worker. We have found, however, that actually describing what makes for effective versus ineffective performance in behavioral terms is more difficult than it seems. It is almost impossible for one person to have a clear and unbiased vision solely on the basis of personal experience. We hope you will come to appreciate the strengths of behavioral job analysis once you have seen it in action. You will find that it involves less work and yields more rewards than might be apparent at first.

♦ WRITING CRITICAL INCIDENTS

Critical incidents are behavior descriptions, but instead of coming from applicants, they come from incumbents, supervisors, executives, and customers. Each incident describes a specific situation that exemplifies effective, average, or ineffective job performance. Good incidents describe exactly what happened as objectively as possible. What led up to the incident? What resulted from it?

Well-written incidents describe rather than evaluate. That is, they describe what happened to make the writer feel, for example, that "this programmer ironed out contradictory program specifications effectively." Well-written incidents avoid such adjectives as *effective, efficient, good, often, sometimes,* and *usually.*

Incidents should not reveal the names of the people involved. They are intended to identify types of behavior, not to single out poor performers for punishment. The following are examples of good critical incidents:

1. A worker reported a burned-out bulb in the early-warning flashing arrow as soon as it malfunctioned, because these bulbs were used heavily and were often out of stock.

2. An operator assigned to the mud-jacking crew first checked key fluid levels, such as gas and oil, and then examined key moving parts to see whether they needed greasing. Consequently, the mud-jacker spent much less time at maintenance for costly repairs.

3. A snowplow operator failed to recognize a railroad crossing on an early morning run. He left his blade down when he went over the tracks, causing damage to the blade that required its replacement.

4. During a congested traffic period at check-in, a frustrated passenger who finally reached the front of the line made a sarcastic comment about the airlines's service. The agent responded with an insult, further irritating the passenger. Soon, several passengers and the agent were engaged in a full-blown shouting match.

5. An agent walking through the airport noticed a woman with two small children and several pieces of luggage with a ticket jacket sticking out of one bag. He offered to help and assisted her to the check-in counter. The passenger complimented a supervisor on the fine service.

Note that a good incident sticks as closely as possible to what happened, avoids judgmental adjectives, and specifies the outcome of the incident. Now that we have shown you what good incidents look like, we will discuss how to go about gathering them.

Incidents can be gathered via written forms, but we recommend face-to-face interviews in most circumstances. Face-to-face interviews return better value especially when (1) access to personnel is easy, (2) incumbents and supervisors share a basic mistrust of new personnel systems, and (3) the organizational level of the person generating the incidents is either low or high.

How many incidents suffice? If the particular job is not one that is analyzed for Appendix A, and if no other source of a behavioral job analysis can be found in the literature, a minimum of 80 to 100 separate, nonredundant incidents should be gathered. If the job overlaps one of the jobs analyzed for Appendix A, or if the literature has a behavioral job analysis for a related job, incidents that tap performance topics not already covered are needed. We recommend a minimum of 10 to 20 incidents per performance topic. Finally, if the job is represented in the Appendix A patterns, we recommend that you gather between 20 to 40 incidents and determine whether they fall clearly into the performance topics outlined for the patterns. Also, show the pattern to managers and incumbents to make sure that it "fits" the local jargon and doesn't leave out something that is unique to your setting.

♦ FORMING PERFORMANCE DIMENSIONS

Once you have gathered the pool of critical incidents, the next step is to form the performance dimensions. Forming these dimensions, or topics, may seem a feat of magic, but it actually involves merely the systematic sorting of the pool of all critical incidents into five to ten groups that contain similar *types* of behavior. (Most jobs have between five and ten performance topics.) Within a particular group, some incidents describe effective performance and others describe ineffective performance, but they all describe the same *type* of behavior. As a finishing step, separate the effective behaviors from the ineffective ones within a given performance topic. This division of a performance dimension's incidents may require further subdivision if some incidents seem more positive or negative than others.

♦ A BEHAVIORAL JOB ANALYSIS EXAMPLE

As an example, consider the job analysis for detail design technician in a county public works department. Table 4.1 gives the performance dimension names and condensed versions of the incidents that fell under each dimension.

Look at the second dimension, "working steadily vs. wasting time." As we sorted the critical incidents for this job, several fell together. One described a technician who stared out the window when there was work to do. Another described a technician who stared at the clock. A third told about a technician who read *People* magazine while work sat waiting. A fourth described someone who asked her supervisor for new work when her current assignment was completed. Another described a time when a technician returned late from lunch because of an extended chess game. Still another described a technician who worked steadily on an assignment until it was completed. Finally, an incident described a technician who walked around the office and interrupted other technicians to talk about hockey, fishing, or football.

These incidents all described how steadily a technician worked. Separating the effective from the ineffective incidents is simple. Further dividing the incidents into subgroups requires a bit more judgment, but it will not make a crucial difference in the quality of the eventual pattern.

The incident regarding the chess game was of slight importance. Those that focused on technicians who wasted their time looking out the window, reading magazines, and the like, formed the next level of importance. Talking on the phone, which ties up a tool others might need, was a separate importance level. Finally, walking around and directly interfering with the work of others was a final level. Most dimensions do not have so many levels. We have illustrated a complex one to show how things can go.

Once we sorted the critical incidents into dimensions, and then again into subgroups within a dimension, we named the performance topics or dimensions. The naming is best done last. Although the natural tendency is to rush toward attaching a name early on in the process, you should resist this approach. Let the content of the incidents be the guide, not your personal ideas of "what it takes to do this job." Otherwise, you may defeat the entire critical incident process.

Table 4.1
Detail Design Technician: Behavior Dimensions and Critical Incidents

1.0 Technical Competence

1. This technician made maximum use of the computer, inputting a set of roadway specifications only once for three analyses... was noticed to seek out necessary information when it wasn't provided, such as requesting extra borings in questionable areas for a soil evaluation... showed good planning in roughing out the detail sizes on a plan sheet to avoid cramming later on.
2. This technician used proper standards on such tasks as establishing sight distances for a roadway profile, setting roadway and shoulder widths, developing storm sewer grades considering utility installations, and making storm sewer runoff calculations.
3. This technician put too many items on a plan sheet... had to redraw pictures of a typical section, even though he was given an example to follow... did not do a complete, finished job on coloring a layout of plan... drew detail of a culvert and roadway profile so lightly that it could not be reproduced... often erased and relocated... left holes in the paper when erasing mistakes... drafted plan sheets that were wrinkled, blotched, and difficult to read.
4. This technician did not provide a flat landing area in the profile at the ramp approach... did not design roadway curves with the proper superelevation... plotted in-place topography from the wrong centerline alignment... developed intersection layouts without considering proper turning movement clearances... inserted the wrong plate when told to insert a certain standard plate into a set of plans... computed a right turn radius alignment tangent to a line parallel to the intersecting road centerline, rather than tangent to a line that is on a taper.

2.0 Working Steadily vs. Wasting Time

1. This technician worked steadily, without interruptions, until he completely finished each assignment... when finished, asked for or found new work to do... willingly accepted opportunities for departmental training whether on county time or his own.
2. This technician made phone calls for personal business, some of them lasting for extended periods.
3. This technician read newspapers and magazines, sat watching the clock or staring out the window when there was work to be done.
4. This technician roamed around the building, striking up conversations with anyone willing to listen on subjects such as fishing, football, etc., disrupting the work of others.

3.0 Detecting vs. Missing Errors

1. This technician was on the lookout for mistakes or unusual data, immediately taking corrective action when mistakes were found...

49

Table 4.1 (continued)

questioned field data that appeared to be incorrect...always set up his computations for ease of checking.

2. This technician did his calculations on many bits of scratch paper, making checking of calculations very difficult, since some of them got lost...missed quantities in transferring from different sheets to the total quantity sheet...did not cross-check plans when revisions were made, allowing some corrections to be missed.

3. This technician deliberately attempted to cover up an error he had made, causing additional time and effort to correct it...fudged a line that didn't fit right when asked to complete a plan sheet.

4.0 Accepting vs. Rejecting Unpleasant Tasks

1. This technician accepted assignments willingly, even those from other sections and those involving menial tasks such as coloring layout, simple drafting, or proofreading.

2. Although this technician performed tasks not to his liking, he wasted time complaining before getting down to work...requested unnecessary additional help to ease his own share of the unpleasant task.

3. This technician found something else to do when given an assignment he didn't like...turned in unusually poor work so that certain tasks would not be assigned to him again...delayed working on an unpleasant job, getting someone else to do it as the deadline approached.

5.0 Maintaining Clean vs. Messy Work Area

1. This technician returned manuals to their proper place...kept manuals up to date by replacing outdated sections...kept his desk orderly so others could find things they needed.

2. This technician left his desk in a mess, making it impossible to find something when it was needed...did not keep his and others' drafting tools clean...misplaced a plan sheet on a small project...often failed to return manuals to the book rack...kept his notes in disorder, making it hard to find things when he was away.

6.0 Getting Along vs. Bickering

1. This technician used tact and acted friendly, even in arguments... was easy to get along with when working in close contact over long projects...was cooperative and flexible in working with other units.

2. This technician bickered about how to accomplish his assignments... argued but would never admit when he was in the wrong.

♦ NAMING PERFORMANCE DIMENSIONS

A performance dimension name should be a concise summary of the content of the incidents that make up the dimension. Avoid, at all costs, one-word dimension names such as "initiative," "attitude," or "efficiency." It is better to let the dimension names grow long than to trim them of real meaning. Consider the dimension names in Table 4.1. They all contain both the positive and the negative sides of the behavioral content. Other job analyses we have done have often had even longer dimension titles to ensure that the incident content is captured. For example, two dimensions from a recent analysis we completed for staff accountants in public accounting firms were "provides clear, organized, complete documentation and working papers *versus* prepares disorganized, confusing written material," and "develops professional, patient, considerate client contacts *versus* is abrasive and intimidating toward clients."

♦ THE JOB ANALYSIS REVIEW

The final step in job analysis is to check the work done so far with supervisors and incumbents to make sure (1) that the incidents are clear and specific, (2) that the incidents belong in the subgroups that were formed, and (3) that no major performance topics were overlooked. The incidents that have been sorted into dimensions and subgroups should be shown to two or three supervisors and two or three incumbents for a final edit and review.

We suggest that this task be accomplished in 30-minute interviews. Begin by having each interviewee review the incidents. The incidents should look something like those in Table 4.1 at this point, but in draft form. Ask the interviewee to point out any incidents that aren't clear or that don't make sense. Also ask the interviewee to point out incidents that don't belong with the other incidents in any particular subgroup.

Once the incidents have been reviewed, ask if any performance topics were overlooked. If most interviewees answer no, the job analysis is complete. If two or three respond that something is missing, have them give some examples of situations that were left out. Flesh out these overlooked areas by questioning the remaining interviewees for incidents. Then decide whether to integrate the overlooked topic with an existing performance dimension or form a new one. Once the reviewers have edited the incidents and verified the completeness of the analysis, the job analysis is complete.

♦ SELF-TEST

1.   What is a critical incident? What determines how many critical incidents should be gathered?
2.   Why is one person's list of traits of top performers less useful than a behavioral job analysis?
3.   What kinds of language are to be avoided in writing critical incidents?
4.   How are performance topics or behavior job dimensions defined?
5.   Why is it better to "go long" on job dimension names rather than to shorten them to just a word or two?

♦ REFERENCES

Flanagan, J.C. 1954. The critical incident technique. *Psychological Bulletin, 51,* 327–358.

Peters, T.J., and Waterman, R.H. 1982. *In search of excellence: Lessons from America's best run companies.* New York: Harper & Row.

CHAPTER FIVE

Ethical and Legal Issues in the Employment Interview

Before we jump into the specifics of the interview itself, we must consider the ethical and legal constraints under which interviewers must operate. Because applicants are generally in a vulnerable position when they are being interviewed, it is important that the interviewer not take advantage of the situation by behaving unethically or by asking questions that violate a person's rights. Let's look at interviewer ethical behavior first.

♦ ETHICAL ISSUES

The interviewer, because of his or her position, holds power over the applicant and should be careful to not abuse that power. The applicant appears at the interview expecting the interviewer to ask questions that generate information that will help determine his or her fitness for a particular job. The interviewer assumes, in turn, that the candidate is willing to have his or her

53

privacy invaded somewhat, so long as the questions pertain to job-related issues. If candidates leave interviews wondering "Why was I asked about my living arrangements and how often I dated?" it is likely that they will feel that their privacy has been invaded for no apparent job-related reason.

Conceivably, situations might arise from specific critical incidents in which such personal questions might be appropriate, but an applicant should be able to understand why such questions are asked and their relevance to the job in question. Interviewers who ask irrelevant personal questions "to get to know the person" are skating on thin ice and may be risking legal problems for their organization. In a court case involving a woman who was denied a position as an urban planner, court records indicated that she had been asked questions in an interview that were not job-related. The woman had been asked how her husband felt about her working and how her family would feel if she was unable to prepare dinner. The court ruled in favor of the woman and she was awarded back pay (Arvey, 1979). Thus, we recommend that interview pattern questions be clearly job-related to avoid possible ethical and legal challenges.

Another dimension of interviewer ethics involves treating all applicants in the same, unbiased manner. Interviewers should identify whatever biases they have and should try to avoid letting these biases influence their perception of an applicant. Prejudging a candidate because he or she went to the wrong school, is of the "wrong" sex, has sloppy handwriting, is a minority group member, is too old (or young), is too short (or tall), or for other job-irrelevant reasons makes a mockery of the interview process. For example, Arvey (1979) suggested that stereotypical beliefs about women in the workforce may bias an interviewer's judgment. Dipboye (cited in Arvey, 1979) suggested that women are often seen as working primarily for extra spending money, are less interested in promotions, and are more content with mundane jobs. Rosen and Jerdee (1976) have also found biases relative to age stereotypes; older people are seen as less productive, less efficient, less motivated, less capable of working under pressure, less innovative, and less creative when compared to younger people. These biases have not generally been supported by empirical research, but they still persist. Similarly, biases based on racial stereotypes are not supported by research or are so minor that they have little practical significance (Arvey, 1979).

If the interview is to be a systematic means of collecting information to make predictions about job behavior, we must treat each applicant in the same way and collect only relevant information. Interviewer "hunches" based on "personal insight" that are not supported by factual data are inappropriate in a cost-effective selection procedure. In this book, we show how interviewers can use job analysis information to generate job-relevant questions, how they can conduct a scientific search for relevant information, and how they can use that information to acquire good prospective employees. Save the unvalidated "clinical insights" and "hunches" for the therapist's couch!

A final ethical issue that we all must face involves our motives in the interview. Some interviewers may have motives other than finding the best candidate for the job, and this confuses the focus of the interview. An interviewer who claims to be "looking for someone who will fit in well" may actually be looking for a "yes man." This interviewer might spend valuable interview time watching the applicant nod and smile appropriately at the interviewer's descriptions of "what it is really like around here." Other interviewers may have a need to exert power over defenseless applicants by making them feel uncomfortable or by asking "tough" questions. If tough questions are asked, it should not be because of a power trip but because they are job-relevant and necessary for determining the candidate's fitness for the job.

The other side of this issue involves the common desire to be liked by other people. One of the authors once worked with an interviewer who spent unusually long periods of time interviewing some applicants who allegedly needed "some support." These hour to hour-and-a-half interviews meant that other interviewers had to do extra work because this interviewer was always busy with an applicant. After a while, it became apparent that the long interviews only occurred when the applicant was overheard to pick up on the interviewer's need for compliments and verbal "stroking." The bottom line of this issue is that interviewers should not allow personal motives to influence their behavior in the interview. If the interview is to be an effective selection tool, it has to be done in an impartial and fair manner. This book presents methods to make the interview a cost-effective procedure, but the conduct of interviewers is solely controlled by the interviewers themselves.

♦ LEGAL ISSUES

In addition to the underlying motives and biases that might affect the interview, there are a number of legal constraints on interviewers' behavior. In the United States, the Equal Employment Opportunity Commission is charged with enforcing Title VII of the Civil Rights Act of 1964, which forbids discrimination in employment on the basis of race, color, religion, sex, or national origin. Title VII as amended applies to state and local governments, educational institutions, employment agencies, labor unions, and all employers with more than 15 employees (Arvey, 1979). In addition, the Age Discrimination in Employment Act of 1967 as amended prohibits discrimination in employment against people between the ages of 40 and 70, unless a person's age is a bona fide occupational qualification.

Other legal constraints on the employment process involve equal pay for substantially similar work regardless of sex (Equal Pay Act of 1963), nondiscrimination and affirmative action in employment for all governmental contractors that receive more than $10,000 per year in contracts (Executive Order 11246), and nondiscrimination and affirmative action in employment for all organizations that will receive government contracts in excess of $2,500 for physically handicapped individuals (Vocational Rehabilitation Act of 1973). These acts, which are enforced by federal agencies, prohibit discrimination against people who are otherwise qualified for a job in question. Individuals may also challenge procedures such as the interview under the Fifth and Fourteenth Amendments to the U.S. Constitution (Arvey, 1979). Thus, almost all employers are required to adhere to nondiscriminatory practices in selection procedures such as the interview.

The Equal Employment Opportunity Commission (EEOC) issued the *Guide to Pre-Employment Inquiries,* which "prohibits the use of all pre-employment inquiries and qualifying factors which disproportionately screen out members of minority groups or members of one sex and are not valid predictors of successful job performance or cannot be justified by 'business necessity'" (Bureau of National Affairs, 1982, p. 9). Thus, if an interview has an adverse impact on groups, or classes, protected by law, the employer must demonstrate the job-relatedness (validity) of the interview and the business necessity for using the interview.

Specific preemployment inquiries that the EEOC encourages employers to scrutinize carefully to avoid adverse impact include the following (Bureau of National Affairs, 1982):

1. *Formal education:* Education requirements adversely affect blacks and other minority groups and generally have not been found to be related to job performance.
2. *Race, color, religion, sex, or national origin:* Such information may be collected for record keeping and affirmative action purposes but cannot be used for personnel decisions.
3. *Height and weight:* Such information adversely affects women and some ethnic groups and should not be used unless the employer can demonstrate job-relatedness.
4. *Marital status, number of children, day care arrangements:* Such information often adversely affects female job applicants.
5. *Ability to speak English:* Unless it's job-related, such information obviously discriminates unfairly against some ethnic groups.
6. *Arrest and conviction records:* Since some minority groups suffer higher arrest rates than whites, arrest records can adversely affect minority groups and should not be queried unless business necessity can be demonstrated. Convictions may be considered if there is a connection between the crime for which the person was convicted and the job.
7. *Military service:* Minority group members are more likely to have general and undesirable discharges, and unless business necessity can be demonstrated, such information should not be used as an absolute bar to employment.
8. *Age:* Individuals between the ages of 40 and 70 cannot be discriminated against simply because of their age.
9. *Financial status:* Questions about home or car ownership, credit history, or bankruptcy can adversely affect minorities.
10. *Weekend work:* Employers are encouraged to accommodate work schedules to the religious practices of their employees.

Readers who require more detailed explanation of legal constraints on employment interviews should consult Arvey (1979) or Ledvinka (1982).

Questions of these types are often included on application blanks or asked in employment interviews. It may be necessary to inquire about some of these areas, but the interviewer should be certain that the questions relate to bona fide occupational qualifications; in other words, they must be truly job-related. Many of these questions are aimed at determining an applicant's credentials, which is just one type of information that is sought in an interview. Since credential-oriented questions tend to encroach on sensitive legal areas, interviewers should keep the legal issues in mind and should carefully scrutinize questions that might lead to legal challenges.

Behavioral description interview questions tend to focus on job behaviors rather than on the credentials that a person may have. The approach to interviewing presented in this book focuses on determining what an applicant has done in the past that will help him or her do well in the position for which he or she is being considered. Questions that inadvertently or otherwise draw out what the candidate has *been* (in terms of ethnic background, sex, age, or religion) do little to tell us what he or she may be able to do in a job in the future. The best predictor of future behavior is past behavior, not simply possession of specific credentials. Thus, we recommend that interviewers avoid questions that dwell on sensitive legal issues and focus, instead, on what the candidate has *done* in the past that can be used to predict his or her future behavior.

♦ SELF-TEST

1.   Why should employment interviewers be particularly sensitive to their general behavior in the interview?

2.   What types of biases might an interviewer have that could affect the outcome of an interview?

3.   What should an interviewer do about a "hunch" that he or she has about an applicant?

4.   What motives might an interviewer have that could influence the types of questions asked in an interview?

5. If an interview has adverse impact on a protected class, what must an employer demonstrate to justify the procedure?

6. Questions about what specific areas may have adverse impact?

♦ REFERENCES

Arvey, R.D. 1979. *Fairness in selecting employees.* Reading, Mass.: Addison-Wesley.

Bureau of National Affairs. 1982. *Fair employment practice manual.* Washington, D.C.: Bureau of National Affairs.

Ledvinka, J. 1982. *Federal regulation of personnel and human resource management.* Boston: Kent.

Rosen, B., and Jerdee, T.H. 1976. The nature of job-related age stereotypes. *Journal of Applied Psychology, 61,* 180–183.

CHAPTER SIX

Forming the Interview Pattern

The basic tools for discovering *what* to ask were covered in Chapter 4, and we sorted out what *not* to ask in Chapter 5. Now you are ready to learn how to write interview questions and how to form them into interview patterns.

There are two underlying themes for writing pattern questions: (1) focusing on performance topics suited to the strengths presented by the interview and (2) writing questions on one job dimension at a time. These two themes reinforce each other to produce an effective set of interview questions.

This book concerns interviewing, not mental testing, simulation, or measuring physical skill. Yet each of these alternative selection strategies has undeniable value in sizing up some aspect of maximum performance by an applicant. By *maximum performance,* we mean the number of problems that are solved or the number of loads of coal that are lifted when a person is highly motivated to do well. We strongly recommend that you include these other sources of information in your effort to improve selection accuracy. Considerable empirical evidence has demonstrated the accuracy and dollar utility of including these other methods when they relate to maximum performance on a given dimension (Hunter and Schmidt, 1983).

The next section discusses the five steps in writing pattern questions for one performance dimension at a time, including what to do when sources of information other than the selection interview are more appropriate and less expensive.

♦ THE QUESTION-WRITING PROCESS

Step One

The first step is to determine the relative importance of maximum versus typical performance for predicting an applicant's on-the-job performance. If how much the applicant *knows* or *can do* is critical to job performance, the dimension tends toward maximum performance. If what the applicant *typically will do* relates more closely to job performance, the dimension tends toward typical performance. Of course, no dimension is purely one way or the other.

Most dimensions are a blend of maximum and typical performance aspects, but many lean toward one or the other. Performance topics that deal with technical skills and knowledge lean toward maximum performance. Performance topics that deal with getting along with others, working hard versus wasting time, and being organized, courteous, or punctual have more to do with typical performance.

Thus, this first step asks you to determine the relative importance of maximum versus typical performance for the dimension in question.

Step Two

If the dimension being assessed leans toward maximum performance, consider skipping this dimension in the interview. Consult an industrial psychologist to find the ability test, job simulation, or psychomotor test that is best suited to the dimension. This will free up the interview for the aspects it measures best, thus increasing the overall accuracy of selection decisions.

You may choose from published cognitive ability tests, job content tests that are developed in-house, job simulations, or psychomotor testing apparatus of varying complexity and expense. Cognitive ability tests have been proved to be valid indicators of performance for a wide range of jobs (Schmidt and Hunter, 1981), and they are cheap. Job content tests developed in-house have the advantage of containing job-relevant material but the drawback of possibly being too easy, too difficult, or too specific.

Often, the critical incidents can help guide the development of effective in-house paper-and-pencil tests. For example, consider the second dimension in the detail design technician job analysis in Chapter 4 (Table 4.1). The incidents detail some knowledge problems for detail design technicians. For a test, technicians or their supervisors could probably write a few questions about standards for establishing sight distances for a roadway profile and the like.

Job simulations involve having applicants perform a sample of tasks that are expected on the job. For a sales job, for example, the applicant might be asked to make a sales presentation after being given some time to study promotional literature. Psychomotor performance tests have been developed for a wide range of physical skill measurement. Various tests of strength, endurance, and agility have been devised—from complex military tracking tasks to the familiar pegs-and-holes task. A complete guide to the availability and application of tests, simulations, and exercises would exceed the scope of this book.

We strongly advise the novice tester to seek professional guidance before rushing into applications of mental or physical ability tests. Too many organizations find themselves in litigation as the result of untrained, hasty decisions to use one test or another. However, managers should not avoid tests just because some companies that have misused them have suffered legal consequences. The costs of dropping valid tests could easily exceed any potential costs of defending their use.

Step Three

For performance dimensions that lean toward typical performance, the next step is to develop question stems based on the critical incidents contained in the pattern. Before actually writing question stems and behavioral probes for a given dimension, review the questions written for previous dimensions, because a specific incident that is probed for one dimension can often yield insight into a second dimension. However, avoid asking the same question stem twice. Instead, insert supplementary questions that cue you to the separate performance dimensions assessed by the specific incident. For example, one common question concerns a recent major accomplishment achieved by the applicant. The incident may bear directly on the job dimension "working steadily versus wasting time," but supplementary questions or probes can also investigate how the applicant handled the interpersonal or planning aspects of the same incident.

The astute reader will by now appreciate the care and attention required for writing clear, effective BD interview patterns. Imagine the difficulty of trying to accomplish the same objectives by the seat of your pants during the interview itself.

Step Four

Now you are ready to begin writing question stems and probes for the pattern. Question stems locate a particular instance from the applicant's past and focus the applicant on that type of event or environment. Probes seek out exactly how the applicant behaved and what the consequences of that behavior were.

The first question stems to be written are those for applicants who have had direct job experience. Scan the incidents listed under the dimension. One way to form question stems is to describe the background section of an actual incident. The probes follow up to see how the applicant behaved in the setting described by the critical incident.

For example, the job analysis for a regional sales representative revealed the performance dimension "establishing new client contacts." One incident from that dimension described a situation in which the salesperson experienced difficulty with a new client contact because the client, a farm implements dealer, was busy at the time. The salesperson persisted, offering to help the dealer load a truck with parts and talking about business when the dealer took a break. That dealer is now a good customer.

We turned that critical incident into a question by asking applicants: "Tell us about the most difficult new client contact you made in the last six months." The probes were:

♦ What was the obstacle you faced?
♦ What did you say when you were stumped?

◆ What did you do to overcome the difficulty?

Notice how we separated the question stem from the probes. The stem fixes a particular time in the applicant's past experience, using the format introduced in Chapter 4. The probes then examine how the applicant behaved in that setting, giving the interviewer the chance to come to an independent assessment of how effective the applicant's behavior was. Phrasing the same stem differently, we might have asked the applicant for the most recent client contact that presented a real challenge.

Step Five

When you have finished writing question stems and probes based directly on the critical incidents, the next step is to develop questions for applicants who have had limited or no direct job experience.

For example, if an applicant for the aforementioned sales position had not had direct sales experience, the question we wrote would not apply. Therefore, the pattern writer must ponder other kinds of situations the applicant is likely to have experienced that get at the same underlying theme. The intention of the incident and the question based on it is to size up the applicant's ingenious persistence and interpersonal sensitivity when making new client contacts. An alternative question might be: "We have all tried to convince someone we did not know well of the merits of a product or idea we were promoting. I would like you to tell me of a time when this was especially tough for you." Then the probes could be:

◆ What made this situation trying?
◆ How did you overcome the obstacles?
◆ What is your relationship to this individual now?

◆ FORMING THE PATTERN FROM THE QUESTIONS

The five steps in the question-writing process will help you accomplish the goal of selecting applicants who will return the maximum performance to the organization. The following three hints will help you accomplish a second goal—securing the maximum number of acceptances of job offers.

First, when you are changing direction in the interview from one major topic to another, start a new line of questions with a self-perception or experience description question. This serves two purposes: (1) it fills in the sketchy outline of the applicant's background provided on the application blank or resume, and (2) it relaxes the applicant by starting with a nonthreatening, nonrevealing topic.

For example, when starting the general topic of recent job experience, you might lead with: "Tell us about your duties and responsibilities at General Gabflab." After that, focus the pattern on specific accomplishments, difficulties, and disappointments experienced at that job. For a managerial position we recently analyzed, one performance topic was "relationship to the community." We started off that section of the pattern by asking the applicants: "Tell us what you feel your strengths are in dealing with the community." We then proceeded to ask for examples of situations in which these strengths were demonstrated, and others in which the strengths were put to their severest test.

Second, avoid the natural tendency to focus on negative behavior. *Always* begin by probing for instances of accomplishment. Follow up with question stems that probe neutrally, such as asking for the last time a particular type of situation came up. Then you can judge whether or not the applicant handled it well. *Only then* should you resort to probing for examples of disappointments (never call them failures or mistakes). People are unused to being asked to recall specific situations of any kind in employment interviews, and they will feel uncomfortable enough at first just trying to remember situations that fit your questions. Try to make it as easy as possible for them by accentuating the positive. As interviewers, you can often learn as much by phrasing a question to dig out "how you overcame this type of problem" as by asking the applicant for an instance of "the last time this type of problem got the best of you." In the latter case, you may draw a blank. In the former, you either may hear about a really effective example of overcoming whatever problem you are probing or you may hear of a weak example of a time when the problem was not really solved. You can be the judge.

Third, completely avoid asking directly for highly loaded

negative experiences. An obvious, extreme example is, "When was the last time you took money from the till?" If the applicant doesn't steal, she or he will surely resent the question. If the applicant has stolen, you will force him or her to lie. A better way to get at negatively loaded material appears in the following example.

In putting together a pattern for hiring a regional sales representative, one performance dimension involved portraying the service being sold accurately and honestly. Exaggerated claims of how much the soils testing service could increase a farmer's yields could cause major problems for the company, since farmers have long memories for "snake-oil" salespeople. Obviously, we could not directly ask, "Tell me about the most outrageous lie you have ever told." Instead, we developed the following question stem: "Sometimes, you can get the customer to do anything but actually sign the contract. Can you think of the last time you needed to stretch the truth a bit to close a difficult sale?" If the applicant responded, "I never stretch the truth," we continued with, "Well, maybe stretching the truth is a bit strong. What I really meant was, when was the last time you painted a rosy picture to close a difficult sale?" As it turned out, in response to this question, many applicants recalled specific examples of times they had deceived customers. Some were relatively minor, and some were examples of the kind of behavior management wished to avoid.

Now that you have done a behavioral job analysis to form the basis for writing pattern questions, gone through the process for turning behavioral job dimensions and their critical incidents into pattern questions, and focused the questions on instances of positive accomplishment rather than relentlessly probing failures and disappointments, you should have a set of questions that are ready to be assembled into a pattern.

If you wish to structure the pattern completely around the job performance dimensions, you are almost done. We suggest, however, that you consider reorganizing the performance topics into groups based on major topics from an applicant's likely experience. For example, common major pattern divisions include: (1) recent direct work experience, (2) job-related work experience, (3) educational experiences, and (4) job-related interpersonal experiences. The sample patterns in Appendix A show both approaches. Sometimes, reorganizing the questions into sections that tie in to the applicant's likely past experiences makes the interview flow better. Jumping from recent job experience to educational experiences and back to interpersonal experiences within a performance dimension can be confusing to applicants and interviewers alike.

♦ WRITING PATTERN QUESTIONS: AN EXAMPLE

This section works partway through the development of a pattern for the detail design technician introduced in the chapter on job analysis (Chapter 4, Table 4.1). We chose this fairly complex job rather than a simple one because it illustrates several points especially well.

The first dimension, "technical competence," leans toward maximum performance. To determine what the technician *can do,* scan the literature for a professionally developed test. The book *Tests* (Sweetland and Keyser, 1983) lists and reviews a wide range of published tests. If a published test is not available, have someone who is skilled in test construction cooperate with technicians to put one together. The test should include questions prompted by the critical incidents. In this way, you can assess how much the applicant knows about detail design drafting. A properly constructed test can often measure technical knowledge better and less expensively than an interview can.

To discover the level of technical competence an applicant *typically* exercises, have the applicant describe a specific challenging project. For an applicant with recent job experience, you might ask: "Tell us about a recent roadway section assignment that you consider challenging. How did you complete the design from the time it was assigned to the time you signed it off?" The probes could be:

- ♦ When were you assigned the project?
- ♦ What specifically was challenging about it?
- ♦ When did you complete the project?
- ♦ What other work were you doing at that time?
- ♦ Did your supervisor comment on the design?
- ♦ What was actually said?

For applicants with no direct working experience, you might ask: "Tell me about the most challenging public works design project you completed in drafting school." Then the probes could be:

- What was the design assignment?
- How did you assemble the information you needed to complete the project?
- How long did the project take to complete?
- Did you hand in the project before the due date?
- Did you get any comments from your instructor in the project?
- What were the comments?
- Did you get any help on this assignment?

A question that would apply to all applicants is: "I would like you to describe a design you found especially difficult." The probes could be:

- What exactly proved to be the toughest obstacle you faced?
- How did you tackle this obstacle?
- How successful were you in overcoming this problem?
- What feedback did you get from peers or your boss?

For the second dimension, "working steadily versus wasting time," the interview remains the prime source of information. As noted in the discussion of step three, some of the questions and probes listed for technical competence can yield insight into how steadily an applicant worked on specific projects. For instance, finding out how much time a technician took to complete a well-known design task indicates how steadily the person worked. To get an idea about whether the applicant looks for new tasks after completing an assignment, you could add a follow-up question: "After you completed that design, what was the next thing you did?" Then the probes could be:

- Were you given that assignment or did you ask around to see what needed doing?
- How often did you obtain new assignments this way?

Some other questions for the "working steadily versus wasting time" dimension are suggested by specific incidents from the job analysis:

From time to time, someone comes along and wants to talk about fishing and football. Tell me about the last time this happened to you.

+ What did you say to this person?
+ How did the person respond?

Tell me about the last time you faced a slack period in the work load.

+ What did you do?
+ When did this happen?
+ About how often do slack periods come up?
+ What was the technician sitting closest to you doing?

Has there ever been a time when you were busy while others in the office weren't?

+ What circumstances led to this?
+ How often has this type of situation come up?

Tell me about the last time you asked for a new assignment.

+ What led up to this incident?
+ How often, on a monthly basis, does this happen?
+ How are assignments generally made in your work group?

One question that gathers information on many performance topics but is especially appropriate for topics based on motivational themes is the "yesterday" question. Those of you who have interviewed are no doubt familiar with its sister question, the "typical day" question. It goes something like this: "Describe a typical day on your most recent job." This is *boring!* Nothing out of the ordinary ever happens on a typical day. Any difficulties or problems that might accidentally get mentioned all have routine solutions. But the story is entirely different if the question is asked about yesterday (or the most recent full working day). Getting detailed, specific responses to such a question requires that the interviewer read, digest, practice, and master the probing skills discussed in later chapters. The question presents a challenging task, but our experience suggests that the rewards justify the effort. The following exchange illustrates the degree of on-the-spot probing that is required:

Interviewer: Now I would like you to tell me what you did yesterday. I know this will try your memory, but we find it useful to get a clear picture of how you do your work. Why don't we start with when you arrived at the office?

Applicant: Yeah, well, I got to work about 7:15.

Interviewer: Seven fifteen sounds early. Does everyone arrive that early?

Applicant: Starting time is 8:00 AM, so no one else was there when I got in yesterday.

Interviewer: How often do you arrive before everyone else?

Applicant: Once in a while, I guess. Yesterday was a fluke. I had to drop my brother off at the airport for an early flight. Normally I get in around 8 and go for coffee with everyone else.

Interviewer: What was the first thing you did when you got in?

Applicant: I went to my desk and sorted through the morning mail drop.

Interviewer: Did anything interesting arrive yesterday?

Applicant: It was mostly advertising and junk mail. There was something about a new type of drafting design software that we were scheduled to implement, so I filed that in my computer file. There was some brochure on our pension plan. Oh yeah, and there was a memo on technical refresher courses put on by the computing staff that sounded interesting.

Interviewer: Sounds good. Have you followed up on that?

Applicant: Not yet, but I put it on my desk somewhere and I will take another look at it in a couple of days.

Interviewer: What time does this take us up to?

Applicant: That took about half an hour.

Interviewer: What did you do to take you up to the time when most other people began arriving?

Applicant: I warmed up the coffeemaker and I guess I straightened out my desk. Sometimes things get pretty scattered in the rush of projects, so it was nice to tidy up a bit.

Interviewer: I see. So who was the first person you talked to?

When probing this question for motivational themes, look for 15-minute coffee breaks that last half an hour and lunch hours that go for two. Ask the applicant separately how many hours he or she typically puts in. Then compare that with the specific data of when that person arrived and left yesterday. Of course, don't forget to check how typical those times are. The applicant who claims to put in a "typical 60-hour week" but who arrives at 8:00 and leaves at 4:00 is telling you something. Comments about asking for assignments and handling slack periods may come up. Thus, patterns and practices on any one day are likely to indicate the general trend, unless something unusual has happened. Probing for how often a specific event occurs will keep you from making leaps of faith based on one day's events. For instance, this applicant's early arrival was found to have a specific cause that was unrelated to motivational level.

Scan the patterns in Appendix A to get more ideas for questions that focus on some specific performance topic. Be creative and original in thinking of approaches for turning the critical incidents into smooth, penetrating interview questions. Most of all, slow down long enough to ask the questions required by the five steps and use the suggestions given in the three hints. If, after following all this sage advice, you are still stumped in developing a pattern for a specific job, write to us. We have never yet met a job we couldn't analyze.

♦ SELF-TEST

1. What is the first step in writing questions for a behavior description interview pattern?

2. Why would you decide *not* to include questions in an interview pattern for a particular performance dimension?

3. What is the difference between maximum and typical performance as it relates to job performance dimensions?

4. What is the purpose of question stems? How are they different from question probes?

5. Under what circumstances should you include opinion and experience description questions?

6. Why should you avoid asking the applicant for several negative experiences in a row?

7. How can the problems with asking questions about highly negative behavior be reduced?

♦ REFERENCES

Hunter, J.E., and Schmidt, F.L. 1983. Quantifying the effects of psychological interventions on employee job performance and workforce productivity. *American Psychologist, 38,* 473–478.

Schmidt, F.L., and Hunter, J.E. 1981. Employment testing: Old theories and new research findings. *American Psychologist, 36,* 1128–1137.

Sweetland, R.C., and Keyser, D.J. 1983. *Tests.* Kansas City, MO: Test Corporation of America.

PART III

Interviewing Skills ♦

♦ *CHAPTER SEVEN*

Establishing and Maintaining Rapport

If you have followed the demanding path laid down so far, you now have a powerful tool for guiding your interview. The behavior description interview pattern zeros in on the kinds of answers you need to separate the high-performing applicants from the mediocre and the potential disasters. But you are not home free yet. Will you get those answers or will they elude your grasp? Will you ask the questions only to be evaded at every turn? How will you handle the dreaded stony silence of a defiant applicant who is annoyed by the way you are trying to probe the dusty corners of the past? All this has happened before. We have seen well-prepared patterns wasted by interviewers who were in too much of a hurry to learn how to use them. If you study the next two chapters, this won't happen to you.

Naturally, we begin with the beginning. This chapter is entirely devoted to getting the interview underway smoothly and then maintaining a positive, professional rapport. Some of you are naturals, and most of what is discussed here will come easy to you. Others will find it more difficult.

♦ FIRST IMPRESSIONS

First impressions are extremely important. Your first impression of the applicant will set the tone for the early stages of the interview. Also, while you are reacting to the applicant, the applicant is reacting to you. We think these first impressions are too important to leave to chance. Interviewers must manage the impressions to create the kind of atmosphere that promotes open, honest answers. Even if you already do most of what we suggest in the next section, you may discover a few new tactics that can have an impact on that fragile first impression.

♦ OPENING THE INTERVIEW

Greeting the Applicant

This is it! You have given a great deal of time and effort to being thoroughly prepared with a set of behavior description pattern questions. Now you need to get the answers to those questions. To do so, you need to strike a balance—with warmth, friendliness, and empathy on one side and objectively obtaining and recording answers to the pattern questions on the other. Too much of one or the other creates problems for the interviewer.

Greet the applicant with a handshake and a smile, and make sure that your nonverbal cues reinforce this friendly, positive greeting. Demonstrate a genuine enthusiasm for the task at hand. As in so many other things, moderation is the key. Avoid both icy frowns and silly grins. Avoid both wistful glances out the window, which indicate a lack of interest, and a hawklike gaze that follows the every pupilary deflection of the applicant. Avoid both the vise grip and the limp wrist. Avoid a thin, flat, monotonic vocal style as carefully as you avoid exaggerated stage diction. We think the phrase *positive professionalism* sums it up pretty well. This is not a social chat with a long-lost buddy; neither is it an inquisition.

The Physical Layout

The physical layout can either assist or detract from the interviewer's efforts to establish rapport. There are two kinds of problems to avoid. First, avoid retreating behind the massive symbols of power that often clutter a manager's office. Conduct the interview over the corner of a desk or over a coffee table. If you are taking notes, make sure you can do it comfortably and naturally. Also, be sure to inform the applicant that you will be taking notes, and explain why. Second, try to ensure that you are not interrupted during the interview. Have your calls held or transferred and insist that you not be interrupted except for urgent crises.

Suggested Behaviors

Taken together, the following behaviors present a profile of an accomplished interviewer greeting an applicant:

1. *Smiling:* The interviewer smiles when eye contact is first established with the applicant; smiles to establish empathy or in response to the applicant's humor; and smiles when delivering a joke or light observation designed to relieve tension.
2. *Shaking hands:* The interviewer extends a hand and delivers a firm, but not crushing, handshake. This procedure is recommended for all combinations of sex of interviewer and sex of interviewee.
3. *Head nodding, verbal approval:* The interviewer indicates interest in the applicant's responses by nodding his or her head and giving short verbal approval, such as "mm-hmm," from time to time, especially after the applicant has emphasized a point.
4. *Eye contact:* The interviewer establishes eye contact with the applicant, especially when asking questions or when the applicant seeks a clarification. The interviewer drops eye contact when finishing up a note or preparing for the next question, or during a calculated pause.
5. *Vocal variation:* The interviewer uses variations in voice loudness and tone to underline important points or requests and to keep communications sounding fresh and genuine.
6. *Postural variation:* The interviewer communicates a relaxed, confident inner feeling through a relaxed, confident, but interested posture once seated; a slight forward

lean when listening to applicant responses; a slight move back when starting a new area of discussion or delivering a tension reliever.

The last two points are not big deals, but varying noticeably from these suggested behaviors can cause the applicant to "clam up."

♦ SMALL TALK

You have shaken the applicant's hand and offered an enthusiastic, "Hello, I'm Tom Janz. Please come in." Now what? It is time for small talk. Again, some people find this easy; some find it awkward and unpleasant. However, if you are nervous, stilted, or embarrassed by small talk, the applicant will feel the same way, and things will be off to a poor start. Unfortunately, some people who believe they are very good at small talk really cause more problems than they are aware of. The following pitfalls with small talk should be avoided.

First is the small talk artist who specializes in some interest that is not generally shared. For example, one interviewer launched into small talk with: "Say, did you catch the match with Seattle last night? Valentine really headed the third goal in perfectly, didn't he?" Some applicants may not be interested in soccer. Others may despise TV sports in general, leading to an icy response like: "I wouldn't know, I gave my TV away a month ago. There is so little worth watching."

Second, avoid small talk that might evoke stressful or negative experiences. One innocent example is: "The weather this past weekend was just superb. What did you do?" The applicant might respond with: "I didn't notice that much. I was at my mother's funeral."

Third, small talk should not go beyond 2 to 3 minutes. Interview time is short enough as it is, and spending 5 minutes on small talk will cut into the time for obtaining the information needed.

Focusing on the positive, one item of small talk that seems to work well in a wide variety of settings is: "Did you have any trouble finding the place?" The response will usually be a sentence or two that will serve to get things off with few hitches. Practice a smile and a head nod as you lean a bit forward to listen attentively to the applicant's response.

♦ THE STRUCTURING STATEMENT

Once you and the applicant have eased into the process and are ready to roll, a structuring statement sets a professional tone for the interview. It also lets the applicant know what will happen and helps put him or her at ease. The following is a model structuring statement:

Shall we get started? My job title here at Scott Industries is Manager, Paint Division. I have been with Scott for about 8 years now, and I've been manager of the paint division for 3 years. As you know, I'm interviewing today for an opening we have for chemical process engineers. I would like to spend the next 30 to 45 minutes going over your background and qualifications. Then I will leave some time at the end to answer your questions about Scott. I will be seeing several applicants, so I hope you won't mind my taping the interview [or taking notes] so that I can keep everyone's qualifications straight. Sound OK? One last thing: the questions we have worked up often ask you to recall a specific event or accomplishment from your past. Sometimes, it takes a bit of time to remember when a particular event happened. Don't feel bad about that. Take your time. We find these specific examples useful in getting to know you better.

You may not use all the components of the model structuring statement, but consider each one carefully. By letting the applicant know what will happen, you allow him or her to be more comfortable. By telling the applicant that you will answer questions toward the end, you avoid annoying questions about pensions and benefits while pursuing your main goal of gathering information. By preparing the applicant for the types of questions you will ask, you make it easier to get clear answers.

♦ PRACTICING YOUR RAPPORT SKILLS

To close this chapter, we have included a sample form for rating the skills needed to open the interview successfully. Ask a friend or colleague to help you assess and improve your interviewing skills. Have that person serve as the interviewee while you play interviewer. Go through the opening from the applicant's knock on the door to the asking of the first question. Then have the "interviewee" rate you on the Rapport Skills Assessment Form. Go over the exercise a few times, perhaps with several people, until you can accomplish the behavioral targets discussed in this chapter.

♦ SELF-TEST

1.   What is the first thing you should do when greeting the applicant?

2.   List four behavior targets for the interviewer during the initial 5 minutes of the interview.

3.   What are two common dangers posed by small talk?

4.   What is the value of a structuring statement in opening the business portion of the interview?

Rapport Skills Assessment Form

	Needs More	About Right	Needs Less
1. Smiling	:____:	:____:	:____:
2. Shaking hands	:____:	:____:	:____:
3. Head nodding	:____:	:____:	:____:
4. Verbal approval ("mm-hmm")	:____:	:____:	:____:
5. Eye contact	:____:	:____:	:____:
6. Vocal variation	:____:	:____:	:____:
7. Postural variation	:____:	:____:	:____:
8. Small talk	:____:	:____:	:____:

A. Physical layout:
[I felt comfortable, important]   7 6 5 4 3 2 1   [uneasy, unimportant]

B. Small talk:
[Helped me to relax, open up]   7 6 5 4 3 2 1   [made me feel nervous]

C. Structuring statement:
[Helped me prepare, be ready]   7 6 5 4 3 2 1   [ordered me around]

CHAPTER EIGHT

Using the Pattern Skillfully

By following the suggestions in Chapter 7 to start the interview off on the right foot, you have stored up good will, which you may need to draw on once the interview gets underway. Some applicants may be able to spill out the details of specific performance events, but most will require some skilled probing. The applicants are not necessarily trying to be deceptive, but most of them have never experienced behavior description questions. What's worse, they will want to come up with answers quickly so that they appear "swift" or "on the ball."

Often, it will take the applicant a bit of time to locate the specific performance event you seek. Therefore, some applicants will respond with opinions; others will simply freeze. You must be able to help them over this initial freeze by using the probing skills suggested in this chapter. If you deal with the first three behavior description questions smoothly, the rest of the interview will flow easily. If you let the applicant "get away" on those first three questions, however, you will have a long, hard battle to salvage enough information to make an informed decision. The skills discussed in this chapter will help you obtain the behavior description answers you need.

♦ PROBING SKILLS AND WHEN TO USE THEM

Fortunately for BD interviewers, many of the problems that typically face users of the unstructured interview are avoided through the interview pattern. Problems such as yes/no questions, leading questions, improper talk ratios, and unwarranted assumptions simply don't arise when you interview from a carefully derived pattern. The pattern makes your job easier, since your job is to get answers to the questions you select from the pattern.

For some applicants, the process will be as easy as asking the questions and recording brief notes on the responses. For many applicants, however, things are not so simple. The following discussion highlights the types of problem behaviors encountered in seeking answers to behavior description questions. We have organized the discussion into subsections for the several types of problem behaviors, with suggested alternatives for handling each type. Once you have acquired and practiced the skills necessary for handling these problem behaviors, you will be ready to tame even the fiercest applicant and make informed, accurate assessments of applicants' future job performance.

Silent Sam

You opened with a handshake and a smile and learned that the applicant didn't have much trouble finding the place. He has just outlined his duties and responsibilities at his last job. You go on:

Interviewer: Focusing on your last job, could you tell me about a particularly challenging assignment you had. What was the assignment?

Applicant: ...

What do you do? The first reaction of most interviewers is to jump in with a follow-up probe or even to move on to the next question. Don't rush the applicant. The first technique for handling Silent Sam is the *calculated pause.* Simply wait a bit—not more than 10 to 15 seconds. That may not sound long, but in an interview it seems like a year. If you take longer than 30 seconds, the applicant may leave, thinking you have fallen asleep. If the wait doesn't work, use another technique, but don't forget the calculated pause.

If the applicant is now squirming a bit and looking uneasy,

use the *you're OK* statement. The *you're OK* statement legitimizes the applicant's freeze and removes the immediate pressure that may be blocking the applicant's memory from finding the specific situation you seek. Your nonverbal and verbal messages should be in tune here. Smile and use an interested tone when delivering the *you're OK* statement. Showing impatience by frowning or an irritated voice inflection defeats the whole purpose. The *you're OK* statement looks like this:

Interviewer: I realize that sometimes it's a bit difficult to dig up these past examples. Most applicants take a moment or two, but that's OK because we find the answers most helpful.

Applicant: Hmmm, well...

Finally, if the applicant still is frozen up, try using the technique of *question restatement*. Restate the question using slightly different wording or emphasis. Try to avoid simply repeating the question. For example:

Interviewer: What we are really getting at is an example from your past job of a time when you were really put to the test. Can you recall a time like that?

Applicant: Well, yes. There was the Wilson Brothers assignment.

and you're off and running.

Betty Bluff

Whereas Silent Sam says nothing when asked a behavior description question, Betty Bluff acts as if such situations happen to everyone but her. Sometimes an applicant really hasn't had an experience such as the one you seek. Effective interviewers probe far enough to make sure that they are not being bluffed. Consider the following actual transcript from a behavior description interview:

Interviewer: Sometimes we are all stumped by a customer question. Can you tell us about the last time you were stumped, and what you did at that time?

Applicant: Hmmm...I just can't think of a time when I was completely stumped. No. I always have something to say.

Question Restatement is the technique of first choice in this case. The applicant has focused on being stumped and having nothing to say, but the intent of the question was to see how the applicant looks for advice when it is necessary. The interviewer followed up:

Interviewer: I realize you always have some kind of reply, but I was interested in situations where you had to get back to the customer after you found out some additional information. None of us always has all the answers.

Applicant: Oh yeah. Sure. There were times when I needed the support of more experienced guys. I had never really gone through the journeyman mechanic phase before moving into sales.

Interviewer: Could you tell us about one of those times?

Notice how the interviewer briefly reviewed what the applicant had said before restating the question. Summarizing before digging in to get the information makes the applicant feel listened to and more willing to come up with the desired information.

The following is another common bluff, again taken from a transcript of a behavior description interview:

Interviewer: To bring this down to the specific, could you tell us about a time when you used this strength to assist you in relating to a community group?

Applicant: Well I use those skills every day—on the job, and at home with my family.

A *calculated pause,* a *you're OK* statement, or a *question restatement* would not be useful here. The applicant obviously tried to dodge the question, and the interviewer must tactfully point out that the evasion won't work. The *sympathetic persistence* technique works well in this situation. It makes the point while removing the barbs from the comment. It goes like this:

Interviewer: I realize it's a bit tough to come up with examples, but could you think of a recent time you used those skills?

Applicant: Well, I don't really know. It is just second nature for me. I use those skills on my children and with my employees just all the time.

Interviewer: Well, if you use them all the time, you must have used them yesterday. Take a moment to recall yesterday and see if you can locate a time that your social strengths helped solve a community relations issue.

You must politely insist on obtaining behavior description answers to the first few BD questions in the pattern. You just can't afford to let the applicant off the hook early. If you do, you may never obtain behavior description answers. Therefore, firmly but politely show that you are on top of your job and know what you want. The answers will come much more easily.

Slippery Sue

Neither Silent Sam or Betty Bluff actually came up with answers to behavior description questions, and the astute interviewer would detect that the questions missed their mark. With Slippery Sue, you do get an answer, but it slips away from the question being asked. The following example comes from the transcript used for Betty Bluff:

Interviewer: Could you tell us about one of the times you were really stumped?

Applicant: When you are really stumped, you look to your senior people for support, your boss or some of the more experienced installation mechanics. It's always a good idea to let the customer know you are seeing to their problems, but you try to diagnose the problem before rushing to a solution.

Here the applicant gave a response, but it described how the applicant *typically* handles being stumped, not a *specific time* when the applicant was actually stumped. This answer is an experience description, not a behavior description. You should be able to tell because the answer is not in the past tense. Also, the answer contains the keyword *always*—a dead giveaway to an experience answer. One technique for nipping Slippery Sue in the bud is called *assumed responsibility*. You take the rap for the applicant's mistake, so it goes down better when you point out that you are not getting the information you need. It goes like this:

Interviewer: I'm sorry. I guess I wasn't clear enough about the answer I wanted. You told me about how you typically handle being stumped, and that's good. What I really wanted to hear about was the last time this happened to you. Can you recall when that was?

Applicant: The last time? Let me see.

Interviewer: That's OK. Take a minute to think back.

Applicant: Oh yeah. The last time was the problem with the freezer case that was showing warning lights when nothing seemed to be wrong....

Here, a combination of *assumed responsibility* and *you're OK* techniques brought out the incident. *Assumed responsibility* should be used only once in an interview, because it wears a bit thin on repetition. Fortunately, applicants usually get the message and get on with the answers you seek. Other techniques suited to the Slippery Sue situation are *question restatement* and *sympathetic persistence*. The basic format is to gently but firmly inform the applicant that you (the interviewer) are not getting the information you want and that you will persist until you do.

By now, you might think that obtaining answers to behavior description questions is like pulling teeth—and sometimes it is. More often, applicants answer the questions directly, but you must be prepared to handle tough applicants when they appear.

◆ SKILLS PRACTICE

We know of only one good way to acquire and refine your interviewing skills—*practice*. Therefore, we suggest that you attempt the following skills practice exercises as warm-ups before trying the techniques in actual interviews.

The Interruption Game

In interviews, it is sometimes necessary for the interviewer to interrupt the applicant. The applicant may be going off on a tangent or stuck in reciting the boring routine of a typical day or some mundane opinion. To execute *sympathetic persistence, question restatement,* or *assumed responsibility,* the interviewer may have to interrupt the applicant. This exercise has the interviewer practice lubricated interruption. By *lubricated,* we mean that the interruption is smooth—that it does not jar the applicant and damage rapport. The Interruption Game requires only two participants. First, one participant takes the role of interviewer and the other takes the role of applicant. Later, the players may switch roles. The interviewer and applicant roles are as follows:

> *Applicant:* Spend as much time as possible talking about your work experience on your *previous* job. Respond to direct requests of the interviewer, but quickly turn the discussion back to your previous job.

> *Interviewer:* Interrupt the applicant and focus his or her responses on *current* work experience. When the applicant begins talking about *previous* work experience, interrupt the answer and refocus him or her on current work experience. You must briefly summarize what the applicant was saying before directing him or her back to current work experience. The order of events should be (1) interrupt, (2) summarize, (3) redirect.

Each player should take from 10 to 15 minutes in each role, until the interruptions are smooth.

The Impossible Applicant Game

This game also involves the two roles of applicant and interviewer. Ten question cards are used by the interviewer, and ten response directive cards are used by the applicant. The applicant then scores the interviewer on how successfully he or she has applied the probing techniques discussed in this chapter. Table 8.1 contains the items for the question cards, and Table 8.2

Table 8.1
The Impossible Applicant Game: Interview Questions

1. Tell me about the most recent time you felt satisfied with something you did on the job.
2. Tell me about a time when you helped someone else solve a problem with which they were having difficulty.
3. Tell me about the most challenging project you completed in the past 6 months.
4. Tell me about a time when you had the most difficulty getting a difficult concept across to someone you were working with.
5. Give me an example of your ability to calm down an irate customer or client.
6. When did you last use your social skills to smooth over a potentially explosive situation between you and your boss?
7. Tell me about the most frustrating time you have experienced in the past 6 months.
8. Tell me about the most recent time you completed a major project. What did you do next?
9. Tell me about the most discouraging feedback you have received in the past year. What did you do about it?
10. Tell me about a time when you needed to make some important decisions quickly. What were they? What happened?

Table 8.2
The Impossible Applicant Game: Applicant Response Directives

1. Silent Sam: Say nothing until the third prod.
2. Betty Bluff: Use the "it happens so often it's hard to think of a specific time" bluff.
3. Betty Bluff: Use the "it was so long ago" bluff.
4. Silent Sam: Respond as though it's on the tip of your tongue but you just can't seem to pin it down. Wait for the second prod.
5. Slippery Sue: Slide into an experience response.
6. Slippery Sue: Turn it into a hypothetical response.
7. Betty Bluff: Angrily criticize the interviewer for asking the question. Claim that the question is "too personal."
8. Slippery Sue: Turn the response into a personal opinion.
9. Slippery Sue: Answer with some statistics or other credentials that are vaguely relevant to the question.
10. Silent Sam: You honestly can't recall the situation the interviewer seeks. Don't give in.

contains the items for the response directive cards. The applicant scores the interviewer on the Probing Skills Assessment Form provided at the end of the chapter.

The game consists of as many rounds as the players can stand. For any round, flip a coin to decide who will take the interviewer role first. That person asks the first five questions from the question deck, and the applicant responds according to the first five directives from the response deck. After five questions, the players can switch roles.

The interviewer's objective is to use the skills described in this chapter most appropriately to obtain a complete answer to each question. The applicant's objective is to follow the role outlined in the response directive card.

The applicant scores the interviewer on the types of answers elicited and on how appropriate the probing techniques were. The interviewers final score is determined by summing the number of BD questions to which the applicant gave BD answers plus the appropriate uses of probes minus inappropriate uses of probes.

♦ MOVING THROUGH THE PATTERN

Three general principles help the interviewer move through the pattern effectively: (1) coverage, (2) balance, and (3) tact. First and foremost, the interviewer must cover the behavior dimensions developed by the job analysis. You will not ask every question on the pattern to every applicant, but each job dimension should be probed to your satisfaction. If one or two of the behavior description questions written for a particular dimension bomb out, make sure that you ask the remaining questions based on that dimension. If the first couple of questions written for a particular dimension tie down that performance topic well, move on to other topics.

For jobs that have one or two job dimensions that stand out as more important than the others, spend more time on questions from those dimensions. The pattern should already reflect the greater importance of key dimensions by containing more questions that are aimed at them.

The second principle is balance. Never move through the pattern in a way that emphasizes challenges, difficulties, disappointments, and failures. Accentuate the positive. Start with stories of successes or accomplishments. Then slide in some questions for the other side of the coin. You should sound almost embarrassed to ask, but to be fair, you want both sides of the picture. Treat stories about problems and difficulties with as much postural and verbal attention as you do stories about successes and accomplishments. Do not dwell on disappointments. Also, do not leap to record a difficulty—you should be taking notes smoothly at all times. The balance of your questions should be 60/40 to 70/30, with the majority on the positive side.

Third, use tact in pursuing a behavior description answer. Be persistent, but know when to give in gracefully. For some specific situations that you are sure the applicant really has experienced, his or her strong personality defenses may interfere with an answer. Don't play therapist and try to break these down. If the applicant has clearly decided not to disclose the event, or if he or she cannot, just drop it gracefully and move on to another area. If the applicant is totally blocked, this behavior in itself should suggest a potentially low assessment on interpersonal skill and customer contact dimensions.

♦ RECORDING APPLICANT RESPONSES

There is little point in systematically digging out behavior description answers to carefully developed pattern questions if they are not retained somehow. Unless you are blessed with a perfect memory, retaining important details means either taking notes or recording the interview.

Although we were initially biased against tape recording interviews, recent experience has suggested several advantages of taping. An interviewer who is freed up from having to take thorough notes is in a better position to move through the pattern skillfully. Also, if management expresses concern over an applicant's score on a key performance dimension, the tape can be reviewed to strengthen the rating on that dimension. Managers can listen to the interview themselves if they show particular concern. Getting applicants to agree to taping the interview has never been a problem for us. The issue is best handled in the structuring statement and should be done openly.

We have sometimes been called upon to evaluate applicants who had been interviewed by others in distant cities. By listening to tapes of these interviews and reviewing brief notes made a few days following the interview, we were able to reach confident conclusions. So far, those conclusions have been borne out by on-the-job performance. Thus, taping can be a useful intermediate step, but it is still necessary to sum up applicants' responses to the pattern questions by taking notes from the tape.

There are two principles of good note taking. First, don't try to record everything. You need the notes only to stimulate your recall of the applicant's response to pattern questions. You need this recall when you assess the applicant's standing on the job dimensions following the interview. Second, keep your notes limited to what the applicant said or did. Avoid recording judgments or hunches that float across your mind during the interview. There will be time for making judgments after the interview is completed.

♦ PRACTICE MAKES PERFECT

You are now ready to begin full-scale practice interviews. When you are practicing, make sure that the person who serves as applicant has some real experiences to probe. In our experience, asking the applicant to "make up" BD answers results in frustration for both the practice interviewer and the practice applicant. Fabricating BD answers turns out to be amazingly difficult—especially if the interviewer is skilled at probing the details of an incident.

The Probing Skills Assessment Form provided here can be used by either the applicant or an observer to structure feedback from your practice interviews. Feedback is crucial; without it, learning and improvement are unlikely. You can also rate your own interviews if you taped them. We recommend that you do so, because you are likely to benefit most from your own criticism— and you will probably be harder on yourself than an observer would be. Have fun—and good luck!

♦ SELF-TEST

1. What is maximum recommended length of a *calculated pause?*

2. Define the following probing techniques: (1) *assumed respon-sibility,* (2) *you're OK,* (3) *sympathetic persistence,* (4) *question restatement.*

3. What is the most obvious reason why applicants have difficulty responding to behavior description questions?

4. Why is it necessary to "lubricate" an interruption? How is it done?

5. What are some key words that can alert you to a Slippery Sue who has converted a behavior description question into an experience answer?

6. Define the three principles that help the interviewer move through the pattern smoothly.

Probing Skills Assessment Form

Questions	Answers				Skills				
	CR	EX	OP	BD	CP	YO	QR	SP	AR
1. _____	__	__	__	__	:__:__:__:__:__:
2. _____	__	__	__	__	:__:__:__:__:__:
3. _____	__	__	__	__	:__:__:__:__:__:
4. _____	__	__	__	__	:__:__:__:__:__:
5. _____	__	__	__	__	:__:__:__:__:__:
6. _____	__	__	__	__	:__:__:__:__:__:
7. _____	__	__	__	__	:__:__:__:__:__:
8. _____	__	__	__	__	:__:__:__:__:__:
9. _____	__	__	__	__	:__:__:__:__:__:
10. _____	__	__	__	__	:__:__:__:__:__:
11. _____	__	__	__	__	:__:__:__:__:__:
12. _____	__	__	__	__	:__:__:__:__:__:
13. _____	__	__	__	__	:__:__:__:__:__:
14. _____	__	__	__	__	:__:__:__:__:__:
15. _____	__	__	__	__	:__:__:__:__:__:

Procedure: Jot down a few words from the question or probe. Then tick off the kind of answer the interviewee provided and score the use of probing skills, as noted below.

Answers: CR=credentials; EX=experiences; OP=opinions; BD=behavior descriptions.

Skills: CP=calculated pause; YO=you're OK; QR=question restatement; SP=sympathetic persistence; AR=assumed responsibility.

Scoring: Score U when the skill was used appropriately; score M when the skill was misused; and score S when the skill should have been tried but was not.

♦ *CHAPTER NINE*

The Recruiting Interview

Some organizations prefer to separate the "telling and selling" of the organization from the information-gathering interview. Others prefer to accomplish both tasks in one sitting. This chapter treats the recruiting function as separate from the information-gathering activities. If you prefer to include the recruiting function in the same interview as your information gathering, we suggest that you do the "telling and selling," according to the suggestions in this chapter, after you have asked all pattern questions. As noted in Chapter 7, the structuring statement should tell the applicant when to ask questions about organizational policies, benefits, and the like—which might stimulate the applicant's interest in the opening. Also, as noted in Chapter 2, we believe that a thorough, fair, probing interview will itself serve to entice highly qualified applicants into accepting offers.

The recruiting interview uses all of the interviewing principles outlined in the preceding chapters, but it differs from other selection interviews in that the interviewer must also "sell" the job and the organization. This added "selling" dimension need not take a lot of time, but how it is handled can make a big difference in how applicants view the organization. When qualified applicants for a job are in short supply, good recruiting interviews can have a tremendous payoff for the organization. In a recruiting interview, the interviewer is still trying to assess the candidate's fitness for a job, but he or she must also present information about the job and the organization that will induce the candidate to want this particular job. Thus, the interviewer is

99

both evaluating the candidate and trying to sell him or her on the merits of the particular job and the organization.

Since recruiting interviews are just the beginning of a selection process that will probably include additional interviews, reference checks, tests, and on-site visits, the organization has ample opportunity to assess candidates who are invited for further screening. Unfortunately, little is known about those who do not "survive" the initial recruiting interview or who decide that they are no longer interested in employment with the organization and decline further contacts. For high-demand jobs, it is imperative that the interviewer leave the candidate with a favorable impression so that the organization can attract the best qualified people. As Rynes and Miller (1983) have pointed out, the impact of the recruiter is great; many candidates cannot distinguish among various job opportunities because of the superficial information exchanged in recruiting interviews. Thus, how the recruiter behaves will certainly alter the applicant's perceptions of the job and the organization. In the often brief recruiting interview, the recruiter and the applicant form impressions of each other that will affect their subsequent decision making. The recruiter, as a representative of the organization, is considered indicative of the type of people in that organization, and the applicant may base his or her decision on impressions formed in a single brief interview.

♦ RECRUITER CHARACTERISTICS

A recent review by Rynes, Heneman, and Schwab (1980) summarized research on the characteristics of recruiters that seem to influence applicants' perceptions and the conduct of recruiting interviews. It has been found that the recruiter has a definite impact on how the applicant views the organization (Glueck, 1973). Rynes et al. (1980) also noted that recruiters are often perceived as being poorly informed—either because they have not read the applicant's resume or because they have little specific information about the type of job for which the applicant is being considered—and that they consequently alienate many applicants. The hectic pace of many recruiting interviews makes it difficult for a recruiter to read each applicant's resume completely, but not doing so appears to defeat the purpose of trying to recruit desirable applicants. Because of the impact of recruiters who do not have specific information, job incumbents who participate in recruiting are likely to be viewed as more credible sources of information than full-time recruiters (Fisher, Ilgen, and Hoyer, 1979).

Other recruiter characteristics that appear to influence applicant perceptions include the recruiter's style of delivery or verbal fluency, age, job title, sex, and race (Rynes et al., 1980). A fluent recruiter who keeps the interview going well and is considered to have a pleasant personality obviously makes more favorable impressions on applicants. Recruiters who are somewhat older than the applicant, but not too old, and who have responsible positions in the organization are also likely to make better impressions (Rogers and Sincoff, 1978). The impact of the sex and race of recruiters has not been extensively investigated, but there is some evidence to indicate that female recruiters are at least as good as male recruiters and that the race of the recruiter may have little effect (Rynes et al., 1980).

♦ APPLICANT PERCEPTIONS

In addition to the desirable characteristics of the recruiter, prompt and frequent follow-up contacts with the applicant appear to increase the likelihood that an applicant will be favorably disposed toward an organization (Rynes et al., 1980). Ivancevich and Donnelly (1971) believe that frequent and personalized contact with applicants—providing them with social reinforcement for their decision to join the organization—is also essential in the interim period between acceptance of the job offer and actually starting the job.

As noted earlier, applicants consider job incumbents more credible sources of job information than full-time recruiters. If incumbents do provide more realistic job information, the question arises whether this realistic job information might actually hinder an organization's ability to attract new employees? Wanous (1980) has argued that realistic job information does not reduce an organization's ability to recruit and that it reduces subsequent turnover, because employees do not have inflated expectations. This has been a difficult conclusion for some to accept, since it seems, intuitively, that telling applicants about the bad as well as the good aspects of a job would have an adverse impact on the perceptions of the total applicant pool. This issue has not been completely resolved, however, and needs more research.

Other issues that influence recruits' perceptions of the organization are the means by which interviews are conducted and the types of additional selection procedures (tests, application blanks, and supporting documents) that are used. Regarding the conduct of recruiting interviews, Rynes et al. (1980) have concluded that applicants dislike interviews in which stress is purposely introduced by the interviewer, both highly structured and highly unstructured interviews, and interviews in which the recruiter dominates the conversation. It appears that applicants like moderately structured interviews that focus on their qualifications for a particular job, rather than discussing irrelevant past work experience or personal issues, which may unduly invade their privacy (Rosenbaum, 1973). In addition, applicants should easily see other selection procedures (tests, and so forth) that are used in the recruiting process as job-related.

♦ SELLING THE JOB AND THE ORGANIZATION

A significant part of the recruitment interview is directed toward providing information to the applicant concerning the job and the organization. An obvious informational need concerns the job itself. Dunnette, Arvey, and Banas (1973) investigated a number of job expectations, including working conditions, recognition, responsibility, supervisory responsibilities, interesting work, variety, accomplishment, ability to use one's own ideas, and using one's own abilities. Of these, interesting work, accomplishment, and using one's own abilities were seen by managers as the most important job characteristics, as were pay and opportunity for advancement. The type of supervision received, job status, and security were also included as variables in the study. In a study of organizational entry preferences,

Strand, Levine, and Montgomery (1981) also included the environmental responsibility of the organization and its fair employment practices as policies of importance. Thus, besides describing the job itself, a recruiter should offer information about the environment in which the job is performed, opportunities for advancement, pay, fringe benefits, and the ethical and environmental posture of the organization.

♦ RECRUITER GUIDELINES

To obtain the best possible recruits in the most efficient manner, the following guidelines for the recruiter were suggested by Gilmore and Ferris (1983):

1. The recruiter should develop a "game plan" for the interview, so that he or she knows what is going to happen in the interview. The recruiter should decide ahead of time what is to be covered in the interview (e.g., rapport building, obtaining information from the applicant, providing information about the job, answering applicant's questions), communicate this plan to the applicant so that he or she knows what is going to happen (this helps reduce anxiety), ask questions that will elicit the desired information, and follow the same format for all applicants to ensure equal treatment.

2. The recruiter should develop this "game plan" on the basis of job-relevant information. If the recruiter doesn't have first-hand knowledge of the job, he or she should seek out appropriate job analysis information. Applicants expect the recruiter to ask job-related questions and to be able to provide specific information about the job (see Chapter 4).

3. The recruiter should read each applicant's resume before the interview. A knowledge of some of the contents of the resume impresses applicants and should help guide the questions asked during the interview. Unless there is some reason to doubt the veracity of information on the resume, it is inefficient to ask the applicant to cover it again in the interview. The time available could be better spent in exploring specific behavior descriptions of job situations.

4. The recruiter should attempt to make the applicant feel at ease in the interview. A cordial greeting, appropriate verbal and nonverbal communication, and concern for the applicant's welfare will help reduce the applicants' anxiety and help them present their best responses. The introduction of undue stress, whether intentional or not, will make the applicant feel uneasy and can differentially disrupt some applicants who might otherwise be good prospects. Even if the stress is not job-related, it can discourage some applicants who may assume that stress is an enduring characteristic of the organization. This is particularly true for applicants who are inexperienced interviewers.

5. The recruiter should conduct the interview so that the applicant does most of the talking. Aside from the period in which the recruiter is providing job-related information to the applicant, the recruiter should be listening. Little information is obtained from an applicant who spends most of the interview nodding and smiling appropriately while the recruiter talks. Recruiters are employed to obtain information from applicants, and that can best be done by asking good questions, letting the applicant talk, and probing when appropriate.

6. The recruiter should develop active listening skills so that he or she can ask probing questions to obtain relevant information and can remember what the applicant said in response to specific questions.

7. The recruiter should provide a clear description of the job and the organization to the prospective employee. This description should be specific and realistic; many applicants will know if they are being oversold. If the job is presented too favorably, the applicant's expectations may be raised unduly, which may lead to later dissatisfaction and increased turnover.

8. The recruiter should develop skills for both observing and providing appropriate nonverbal communication. Applicants provide considerable information through their nonverbal behavior, which can be helpful to a recruiter, particularly when the applicant is being considered for a job in which considerable face-to-face contact is required. The other side of the nonverbal communication process is the nonverbal cues the recruiter gives the applicant. Eye contact, gestures, and posture can communicate considerable information to an applicant about the recruiter's interest (see Chapter 7).

9. The recruiter should record observations about the applicant during the interview, so that information about one appli-

cant is not confused with that about another. These notes will be helpful when the recruiter attempts to make judgments about the applicant. Only by careful recording of information can a recruiter hope to keep the information about several applicants from becoming a confusing collection of impressions.

10. The recruiter should be aware of current legal and ethical issues surrounding the interview process. Careful planning of questions can avoid undue intrusion on an applicant's privacy and can help avoid potential legal difficulties. Interviewers who "fly by the seat of their pants" are asking for trouble and may offend applicants who are good prospective employees.

11. Finally, the recruiter should not allow too much time to pass between contacts with applicants. Applicants who have frequent contacts with a prospective employer are less likely to accept other positions, and it is simply good public relations to keep applicants informed of what is happening concerning their chances of employment.

Thus, the job of the recruiter, if it is done well, is not easy and should not be taken lightly. The recruiter is the applicant's first contact with an organization, and his or her impact on the applicant is enduring. To attract high-quality applicants, the recruiting process must be conducted in a professional manner.

During the recruiting interview, considerable information is exchanged between the recruiter who represents an organization and the applicant who is seeking employment. This exchange of information—the "sizing up" that occurs—has considerable impact on the organization's ability to recruit new human resources and on the applicant's potential career. It is important that it be done well!

♦ A SAMPLE RECRUITING INTERVIEW

To close this chapter, we offer an excerpt of a recruiting interview to illustrate how the recruiter can "sell" the job and the organization to the applicant. The following is a sample of a recruiter's "pitch":

Well, Tom, you've answered the questions I had. Now I'd like to tell you about our company and the job for which you are being considered.... First, XYZ Corporation, as you probably know, is a major manufacturer of data processing equipment. We have a variety of facilities in the United States and Canada, with subsidiaries in a number of other countries. We have primarily focused on the development of microprocessor-based computer systems for use in accounting, word processing, and telecommunications. If you should come to work for us, you would probably be assigned to either our research and development laboratory in Austin, Texas, or our development laboratory at our manufacturing facility in Minneapolis. At either place, you will find a number of bright engineers like yourself who are involved in what I think are very challenging work assignments. After a brief orientation period, probably 6 to 8 weeks, you and your manager will jointly decide what projects would be best for you.

The company is very committed to using peoples' skills on the type of work they want to do. You will have the opportunity to use your abilities to accomplish specific objectives. Of course, the projects that you work on at first will have some corporate relevance, but if you prove yourself, you will be given more latitude to pursue your unique interests. Since we are in a high-tech field, innovations come fast, and we reward those who are productive with promotions, salary, and work assignments. Not everyone advances extremely fast, but our engineers are typically considered for a senior position within five years.

Now let me tell you about the company in general. This brochure will explain our corporate human resources policy, training possibilities, fringe benefits, and vacation policies. I think you'll find that we are a very progressive company.

The company is committed to development of each employee's capabilities and believes in the dignity of each person. All employees, regardless of race or sex, are given every opportunity to develop themselves. Now, that sounds like very good public relations verbiage, but it really is true in our company. The company recognizes that the only way it can remain competitive is to have dedicated and competent employees. I have been very pleased with how I've been treated, and no employee can say the company does not support them.

I could tell you a lot more about us, but I'm not certain what you would like to know. Let's stop here and give you an opportunity to ask questions about us.

At this point, the interviewer can answer specific questions raised by the applicant. Once the questions have been answered, the interviewer should close the interview.

Note that the interviewer presented a positive but realistic picture of the proposed job. Challenging work that allows for accomplishment of meaningful objectives and is recognized by salary and promotion was described. However, the recruiter did not paint an overly favorable picture of the job.

Also, by allowing the applicant to raise questions, the recruiter can address specific concerns. A brochure or printed matter can answer many of the applicant's questions and gives him or her something to review after the interview.

♦ SELF-TEST

1. In what ways does the recruiting interview differ from the usual in-house employment interview?

2. What can a recruiter do before the interview to ensure that a candidate will be favorably impressed?

3. Why is it important to give the candidate realistic job information in the recruiting process?

4. What type of information about the job should be provided to the candidate?

♦ REFERENCES

Dunnette, M.D., Arvey, R.D., and Banas, P.A. 1973. Why do they leave? *Personnel, 50,* 25–39.

Fisher, C., Ilgen, D., and Hoyer, W. 1979. Source credibility, information favorability, and job offer acceptance. *Academy of Management Journal, 22,* 94-103.

Gilmore, D.C., and Ferris, G.R. 1983. The recruitment interview. In K.M. Rowland, G.R. Ferris, and J.L. Sherman (Eds.), *Current issues in personnel management.* Boston: Allyn & Bacon.

Glueck, W. 1973. Recruiters and executives: How do they affect job choice? *Journal of College Placement, 34,* 77-78.

Ivancevich, J.M., and Donnelly, J.H. 1971. Job offer acceptance behavior and reinforcement. *Journal of Applied Psychology, 55,* 119-122.

Rogers, D., and Sincoff, M. 1978. Favorable impression characteristics of the recruitment interviewer. *Personnel Psychology, 31,* 495-504.

Rosenbaum, B.L. 1973. Attitudes toward invasion of privacy in the personnel selection process and job applicant demographic and personality correlates. *Journal of Applied Psychology, 58,* 333-338.

Rynes, S.L., Heneman, H.G., and Schwab, D.P. 1980. Individual reactions to organizational recruiting: A review. *Personnel Psychology, 33,* 529-542.

Rynes, S.L., and Miller, H.E. 1983. Recruiter and job influences on candidates for employment. *Journal of Applied Psychology, 68,* 147-154.

Strand, R., Levine, R., and Montgomery, D. 1981. Organizational entry preferences based upon social and personnel policies: An information integration perspective. *Organizational Behavior and Human Performance, 27,* 50-68.

Wanous, J.P. 1980. *Organizational entry.* Reading, MA: Addison-Wesley.

PART IV

Assessment ♦

CHAPTER TEN

Selection Decision Making

The interviewer has reached the end of the pattern, has performed the appropriate recruiting tasks, and has informed the applicant of what happens next; the applicant departs. Several pages of scribbled notes lie on the table. Two crucial steps remain before the interviewer can complete accept or reject decisions about applicants. This placement of the decision about applicants at the end of the process, not in the middle of the interview, is another key difference between behavior description interviewing and traditional, unstructured interviews.

According to Ed Webster's (1982) recent book on interviewing, the selection decision belongs in the interview. We agree with Webster that the decision is the *purpose* of the interview, but we strongly disagree that it should be *part* of the interview. The interview provides information that leads up to the decision, but the interview itself is not the place for making the decision. Webster (1982) has clearly demonstrated in his own research the many pitfalls of making decisions in the interview itself. When they are forced to make decisions within the interview, interviewers are in a rush to make the decisions, and they often make up their minds very early on—within the first 4 minutes. Information from the application blank has been shown to wield undue influence and to get the interview off on either a strongly positive or strongly negative tack. Sometimes it never returns to

111

a fairminded course, turning instead into a witch hunt for negative information. The solution is simple—take the decision out of the interview. This chapter applies what is known about accurately assessing people against clear performance topics once the interview is complete to making the accept/reject decision on a logical basis.

We realize that after all we have asked of you so far, you are getting impatient to go out and make decisions. You began by developing or refining one of our patterns to suit your individual job. You investigated the equal opportunity implications of your questions to ensure maximum compliance with EEOC guidelines. You practiced your skills at digging out behavior description answers to the pattern questions. You learned how to interrupt applicants with an easy, lubricated style. You set up your own system for taking notes. You organized your "tell and sell" function at the end of the interview. Now, you stand the best chance of reaching high-quality decisions if you stick it out through this final, brief chapter that fills out the BD approach.

♦ ASSESSMENT TOOLS

Assessing the applicant involves assigning numbers to your evaluation of the applicant's position in the behaviorally defined dimensions of the job. We suggest that you start with a rating format that has five applicant categories on each job dimension, such as the format of the sample Applicant Assessment Form provided here. As you can see, each category corresponds to one-fifth of the performance distribution on each dimension. A 5 rating means that an applicant places in the top 20 percent of all applicants on this dimension. A 4 puts the applicant in the 60- to 80-percent range. A 3 puts the applicant squarely in the average category. A 2 places the applicant below average, in the 20- to 40-percent range. A 1 places the applicant in the bottom 20 percent.

♦ ASSESSMENT PROCEDURES

At first, placing applicants into the five categories will be difficult. Against whom do you compare them? In fact, however,

Applicant Assessment Form

Name: _____

Position: _____

Date of interview: _____

Interviewer: _____

Dimension	1 Bottom 20%	2 Next 20%	3 Middle 20%	4 Next 20%	5 Top 20%
1	I_____I_____I_____I_____I_____I
2	I_____I_____I_____I_____I_____I
3	I_____I_____I_____I_____I_____I
4	I_____I_____I_____I_____I_____I
5	I_____I_____I_____I_____I_____I
6	I_____I_____I_____I_____I_____I
7	I_____I_____I_____I_____I_____I
8	I_____I_____I_____I_____I_____I
9	I_____I_____I_____I_____I_____I
10	I_____I_____I_____I_____I_____I
Total		I_____I			

it will be easier than it appears. Some applicants clearly shine, others are obviously mediocre, and still others are dreadful on particular dimensions. As the novice assessor gains practice, the process will become easier. Also, you can check with other decision makers about how they would rate a particular incident on a particular dimension. We suggest following four steps in the assessment process.

Step One

As soon as your interview notes are completed, fill in an Applicant Assessment Form for the applicant. If the interviews were taped, this may be done some time after the interview itself.

Step Two

When you make the ratings, deal with one dimension at a time. Start with the first dimension and review your notes. Pay special attention to responses to questions that were targeted for that dimension. At the same time, be on the alert for any other responses that bear on the dimension in question. After selecting a rating, review in your own mind what the applicant told you that led you to choose that number.

Step Three

When all interviews for a particular position are complete, review your assessments along with the notes from each interview. Make sure you have been fair in assigning the same values to similar applicant responses. Make direct comparisons of low and high scorers on key dimensions to ensure that their behavior justifies their ratings. For example, if you gave John B. a 4 and Mary F. a 2 on dimension two, check over your notes to make sure you have good behavioral evidence of John's superiority on that dimension.

Step Four

If you are not the only person conducting interviews for a particular position, get together with the other interviewers after several interviews have been completed. Compare notes, and see how other interviewers rate common answers to the pattern questions. Make sure that you share a common viewpoint regarding the performance implications of specific stories that surface repeatedly. Summarize your meeting by listing common answers and indicating the degree of positive or negative performance impact of each story. Use these stories as benchmarks when you make your own assessments in the future.

♦ RATING ERRORS AND HOW TO AVOID THEM

Regardless of how well intentioned we are as assessors, it is possible to slide into common rating errors that can become bad habits. By *rating errors,* we mean ways of consistently messing up the numbers assigned to applicants on the behavior dimensions. One way to check up on your rating quality is to scan all the ratings you have made within a given period. It should then be obvious whether you have committed or avoided rating errors. After you have completed 10 to 20 interviews, put all your rating sheets together and see how they stack up in regard to the following common errors.

Elevation Error

One common rating error involves rating all applicants either too high or too low over all dimensions. When you look over your ratings, is everyone in the top three categories? If so, you have obviously been too lenient. If everyone is rated 3 or lower, you have been too tough. No one expects that for every sample of applicants there will be exactly 20 percent in each of the five categories, but big differences from the 20 percent definition should alert you to the possibility of a persistent elevation error, which can lower assessment accuracy. To correct this error, review your notes and assessments and bring the overused and underused categories more into line where justified.

Dispersion Error

Dispersion error also shows up in how the applicants were assigned to categories. The common problem here involves rating all applicants right down the middle. The novice interviewer/

assessor often finds it hard to justify placing applicants in the top or bottom 20 percent categories and finds refuge in the middle.

If all your ratings are 2's, 3's, or 4's, review your notes and try to find more low and high scores. Take a stand when an applicant has provided evidence for a low rating or merits a 5.

Halo Error

Halo error can seriously detract from rating quality, but detecting it requires a closer look. Halo error occurs when a person who is outstanding on one dimension is consequently overrated on other dimensions. Similarly, the error occurs when an applicant who is dreadful on one dimension is therefore underrated on other dimensions.

Rating applicants on one dimension at a time helps reduce the severity of halo error. Focus all your attention on the dimension being rated. Furthermore, when an applicant stands out on one dimension, be sure to question the other dimensions carefully, thus avoiding the halo trap. Conversely, when an applicant merits a low score on one dimension, make sure low scores on other dimensions follow strictly from the behavior on those dimensions. Avoid carrying over the strong impression left by the first dimension.

♦ FINAL DECISION MAKING

This final step in the BD process, though important, may seem a bit anticlimatic. If you carefully follow the steps we have suggested so far, the actual decision will be largely a clerical task. The applicants with the highest total scores are given offers. If any offers are turned down, the person with the next highest score is chosen. If there are ties, the notes are reviewed and the applicants are rerated to decide who gets the offer.

You see, all the work that was put in during the job analysis, patterning, training, recording, and assessing steps has made the decision a simple, straightforward process. You must be strong, however. If you give in to your gut feelings now—hiring an applicant you "really liked" even though that person did not make it into the top-scoring group—you have defeated the entire behavior description process.

For most jobs and most hiring situations, the decision is as simple as adding up the dimension scores and recommending the applicants with the highest scores. However, two complicating situations do crop up at times: (1) some dimensions are much more important to overall job performance than others, and (2) decisions may be needed about some applicants before all applicants are interviewed.

Weighting Job Dimensions

If the behavior dimensions substantially differ in their importance on the job, then the more important ones should get more weight than the less important ones. One simple way to determine the weights involves spreading 100 points across the dimensions such that the number of points assigned to a dimension reflects its importance. If several interviewers are assigned to the same group of jobs, get together to set the weights. Also, check out the spread of points with supervisors and workers to make sure you emphasized the right dimensions.

To find a total score, multiply an applicant's score on the dimension by the number of points assigned to that dimension. The total score for the applicant is then the sum of the dimension scores multiplied by the dimension weights. The process is simpler than it sounds, as shown in the following example based on the detail design job analysis in Chapter 5. We have computed the total score for Jack, a mythical applicant, as follows:

Dimension	Score	Weight	Cumulative Total
Technical competence	4	25	100
Working steadily	3	25	175
Checking errors	2	15	205
Accepting unpleasant tasks	4	15	265
Maintaining clean area	4	10	305
Getting along	2	10	325

Jack's total score is 325. Obviously, an applicant who is stronger in checking errors and getting along would have a better chance than Jack.

There are more complicated and more sophisticated ways to derive total scores, but research has shown that it is difficult to beat this simple approach. Furthermore, unless some dimensions are at least two to three times as important as some others, you are better off just adding up the unweighted dimension scores. We don't believe in complexity for complexity's sake. There must be a payoff.

Setting Minimum Cutting Scores

The second possible complication occurs when it is necessary to make decisions about some applicants before all applicants are interviewed. In this case, it is not possible to award the offers to the applicants with the highest total scores. You can handle this situation in one of two ways.

Group competitions
The simplest way to solve this problem is to break the hiring stream into several groups. Competition periods can be based on business cycles or can be scheduled quarterly. In this way, the applicants with the highest scores within any competition period receive the offers. When possible, this simple answer remains the best.

Setting cutting scores
A cutting score is simply a number that is assigned as a minimum acceptable score; applicants whose total scores fall below the cutting score are not considered. We find setting cutting scores a tricky business at the best of times. Cutting scores must be carefully and frequently reviewed, since optimal cutting scores vary with changing conditions, such as the quality and quantity of applicants available for the opening.

If you have to set cutting scores to maintain a steady stream of qualified recruits for entry-level positions, here are some suggestions for doing it well. First, set two cutting scores. Form the bottom cutting score by summing minimally acceptable performance ratings for each dimension. Then form the top cutting score by summing the rating you think the typical top-third performer would get on each dimension. If an applicant falls below the bottom cutting score, cut that person from further consideration. If the applicant falls above the top cutting score, make an offer.

If an applicant falls between the two cutting scores, either hire the applicant on a clearly probationary basis or put the offer on hold until more applicants are interviewed.

Second, in setting the top and bottom cutting scores, take a dimension at a time. Look at the first dimension and determine what kind of behavior leads to a 1, 2, or 3. What is minimally acceptable to you? This forms the bottom cutting score for dimension one. Then consider what kind of behavior you would expect from a top-third performer. What number would that behavior merit? This forms the top cutting score for dimension one. Do the same for the rest of the dimensions and add up the numbers for the bottom and top cutting scores over all dimensions. If you are also using unequal weights, multiply the cutting score number by the weight to arrive at the cutting score total. Obviously, this process is highly subjective, so we prefer the direct competition approach.

♦ CONCLUSION

We began this chapter by encouraging the reader to follow the BD process through to completion. It makes little sense to carefully develop behavior-based job dimensions and a BD interview pattern and polish up questioning skills only to make the hiring decision itself prematurely. A careful assessment of each applicant on each behavior dimension completes the BD process.

We began this book with promises of rewards and a warning about hard work. At this point, the hard work should be almost over. The rewards will accumulate with every interviewee who leaves respecting the quality of the interview and with every hire who performs effectively.

♦ SELF-TEST

1. Why is it important to assess an applicant on one dimension at a time?

2. What are elevation errors, and how can you detect them?

3. What is the remedy for dispersion errors?

4. How do you make the final decision in the simplest case?

5. Why are cutting scores not recommended unless absolutely necessary?

6. Define top and bottom cutting scores.

♦ REFERENCE

Webster, E.C. 1982. *The employment interview: A social judgment process.* Schomberg, Ontario: S.I.P. Publications.

Behavior Description Interview Patterns

The following patterns can be used just as they are for training, but we suggest that you verify their completeness and local applicability before using them in actual interviews. The time and effort spent in adding local phrases and ensuring the completeness of the pattern will pay off in two ways. First, it will show your people that their views merit consideration in all important human resource issues. Second, it will increase the job relevance of the patterns, thus supporting job-relevance claims in the minds of applicants and lawyers alike.

The patterns are provided here in alphabetical order by job title. Within each pattern, the interview question numbers cross-reference the relevant behavior dimensions. Twelve of the patterns break the interview into sections according to general experience topics; four patterns are divided strictly by behavior dimensions.

♦ Bank Teller

♦ BEHAVIOR DIMENSIONS

1. Is pleasant, courteous, helpful to all customers *versus* is curt, rude or insulting to difficult customers.
2. Works steadily, is timely *versus* wastes time, is tardy.
3. Checks for errors, omissions *versus* makes mistakes.
4. Contributes to pleasant, cooperative relations with peers *versus* argues, bickers, causes resentment and dissension.
5. Reports problems or difficulties to the supervisor promptly *versus* hides problems or blames others.

♦ INTERVIEW QUESTIONS

0.1 Let's begin by having you fill me in on your duties and responsibilities at your most recent job that are related to our opening for a teller position.

1.1 I'm sure you realize how important it is to serve customers cheerfully and pleasantly. Tell me about the nicest compliment you received when serving a customer.

- ♦ What did the customer want?
- ♦ Do you remember what you said at the time?
- ♦ What did the customer say when he or she complimented you?
- ♦ Did the customer tell anyone else?
- ♦ How often did this type of event come up last year?
- ♦ Tell me about another one. [repeat probes]

1.2 Not all customers are that nice. Sometimes customers are irritating or rude. Tell me about the most irritating customer you have had to deal with.

122

- When did this happen?
- What did the person do that was irritating?
- What did you say in response?
- How did you overcome the person's rudeness?
- Was the person satisfied when he or she left?
- Did the person say anything to your boss? What?
- How often did this kind of customer show up?
- Tell me about another one. [repeat probes]

1.3 Everyone has said something to a customer, especially the difficult ones, that they wish they hadn't said. What is the thing you most regretted saying to a customer?

- What led up to this particular event?
- What happened after that?
- Did you take any steps to make sure it didn't happen again?
- What were they? Was it effective?

0.2 Let's move on from your customer relations. Now I'd like to find out a bit about your success in catching errors. What do you do that helps you pick out mistakes?

3.1 Can you think of the mistake you picked out on your last job that saved the company the most money?

- When did that happen?
- What was the mistake? Who was responsible?
- Was the mistake avoidable? How?
- What did you do to correct the mistake?
- What did you do to avoid it in the future?
- When was the next time this kind of mistake came up?

3.2 We can all think of the one that got away—the mistake we would most like the chance to do over. Tell me about the mistake you would most like to do over.

- What was your responsibility in this instance?
- What actually happened? For how long?
- What did your boss say about this mistake?
- What did you do to avoid this in future?
- Did this kind of mistake ever happen again?

5.1   Another important quality of a bank teller is pointing out problems and difficulties promptly to your supervisor. Tell me about a time when pointing out a problem or difficulty you were having helped out you and your company a lot.

- ♦ When did you go to your supervisor?
- ♦ What did you say about the problem?
- ♦ What did the supervisor do that was helpful?
- ♦ What kinds of problems did this prevent?
- ♦ How often did this kind of situation come up last year?

5.2   We all have one story about a time when we put off talking to our boss about something. Tell me about the time you were most reluctant to go and talk with your supervisor, even though you knew you should.

- ♦ What were the circumstances surrounding this event?
- ♦ What restrained you from talking with your supervisor?
- ♦ When did you actually talk to your boss?
- ♦ When did you first conclude that you should check this out with your supervisor?
- ♦ What were the consequences of waiting?

0.3   One thing in the banking business that is common to many jobs is that customer demand has its ups and downs. Sometimes you are very busy and other times it slacks off. How did you generally prepare for the peak rushes on your last job?

2.1   Tell me about the busiest time you had on your last job.

- ♦ What did you do to prepare yourself for the onslaught?
- ♦ How did you know what to expect?
- ♦ How did your preparations pay off during the rush?
- ♦ Did your boss ever mention anything about your ability to handle a rush? What was said?

2.2   Just as there are busy times, there are also slack times. Tell me about the most recent slack time you faced.

- ♦ When did this happen?
- ♦ How slack was it compared to a normal flow?
- ♦ What did you do during this period?
- ♦ What were your peers doing during this time?

♦ Did you ever ask for assignments during slack times?
♦ [If yes] Tell me about a time when you did.

0.4 I'd like to close by asking a few questions about how well you got along with your co-workers. What are some of your strengths in dealing with your co-workers?

4.1 Tell me about the last time you used one of those strengths to smooth over an argument you had with a co-worker.

♦ What was the problem about?
♦ What did you say when you approached the co-worker?
♦ When did you approach the co-worker about the problem?
♦ How did the co-worker respond to you?
♦ What was the eventual resolution of the problem?
♦ When was the next time this problem surfaced again?

4.2 Tell me about a time when you helped a co-worker with learning a new task or solving a problem.

♦ What was the task you helped the co-worker with?
♦ How did you learn that the co-worker needed help?
♦ How did you explain the answer?
♦ What did the co-worker do?
♦ How did the co-worker feel about your help?
♦ How do you know the co-worker felt that way?

4.3 Tell me about the most trying time you have had with a co-worker. We all experience some unpleasant times with our peers.

♦ What led up to this event?
♦ How did you approach the situation?
♦ What did you say?
♦ What did the co-worker say in response?

♦ Cashier Supervisor

♦ BEHAVIOR DIMENSIONS

1. Follows *versus* ignores store rules and regulations.
2. Communicates clearly, attentively, and politely to all customers *versus* is inattentive or rude with irritable customers.
3. Checks work thoroughly for mistakes *versus* assumes things are OK.
4. Maintains attendance, informs boss of valid absence *versus* takes extra "long weekends," informs boss at last minute or not at all.
5. Shows initiative and creativity in trying improvements in procedures *versus* prefers doing it "the old way."
6. Trains new cashiers by showing procedures and patiently explaining difficult details until clear *versus* leaves new cashiers on their own, becomes irritated by slow learners.

♦ INTERVIEW QUESTIONS

0.1 I would like to begin by having you review your on-the-job experience that makes you suited to our opening.

[If applicant has cashier supervisor experience]

3.1 Many cashier supervisors check over a few items before starting a shift. Tell me about how you started your most recent shift. What checks did you perform?

- ♦ When was your most recent shift?
- ♦ When did you arrive to begin the shift?
- ♦ When did the shift itself start?
- ♦ What was the first thing you checked?
- ♦ Why are these checks necessary?

[If applicant has only cashier experience]

3.1 Some cashiers check over a few items before they start each shift. Tell me how you started your most recent shift. What checks did you perform?

  ♦ [Same probes]

3.2 Tell me about a time that your startup check really saved you a lot of trouble later on.
  ♦ When did this happen?
  ♦ What problem did the check pick up?
  ♦ What could have happened if you had not checked?
  ♦ What steps did you take to avoid this problem?
  ♦ About how often did this type of problem come up?

3.3 No matter how carefully we check, there is always the one that got away. Tell me about the biggest slip that happened on your most recent job.
  ♦ What information was missed?
  ♦ What were the consequences for the company?
  ♦ What steps did you take to avoid this type of problem?
  ♦ Did this type of problem ever come up again?
  ♦ How did you handle it in that case?
  ♦ What did your boss say to you about this mistake?

1.1 Let's move one to another topic. Tell me about the most recent time the store experienced a product shortage. How did you handle it?
  ♦ What was the background to the shortage?
  ♦ What did you say when the customer approached you?
  ♦ What steps did you take to check on the order?
  ♦ How often did shortages occur?
  ♦ Did you ever handle a shortage differently? How?

0.2 Teaching less experienced cashiers new procedures is one aspect of the job. What skills do you have that make you suited for this task?

6.1 Tell me about the time when you feel you were most effective in helping a new cashier learn something.

- When did this learning take place?
- What was the procedure you taught?
- How did you teach the procedure?
- How long did it take to get it across?
- How well did the new person perform?
- How often did you help new cashiers learn a procedure?

6.2   Sometimes people just don't seem to catch on when you are teaching something new to them. Tell me about the most frustrating time you experienced trying to teach a new procedure.

- [Same probes as 6.1]
- How often did this type of incident come up last year?
- What steps did you take to prevent this type of event from coming up again?

3.4   Balancing the cash bag is always the bottom line for cashier positions, but bags can't always balance. Tell me about the time your experience helped you discover why your bag didn't balance.

- What was the actual imbalance?
- What led to it?
- How did you discover the reason?
- Why would it have been tough for others to figure it out?
- How often have imbalances occurred in the past 6 months?
- How many times were you unable to reconcile them?

3.5   Tell me about the biggest unreconcilable balance.

- What was the amount?
- When did this occur?
- What are the likely reasons for it?
- What steps did you take to improve your balance record?

0.4   Now, please describe your record of attendance in general.

4.1   We all have to miss some days for good reasons. Tell me about the most recent time that you needed time off.

- What was the reason for the absence?
- When did you first know you would not go in that day?
- When did you inform your boss of your absence?
- How many absences did you need last year?

0.5   These next questions try to assess your supervisory qualifications. What are some strengths you have that make you suited to supervision?

5.1   Supervisory positions require that people take the initiative to go beyond what they are told to do. Tell me about a time when you showed the most initiative.

- ◆   What did you do that was beyond your normal duties?
- ◆   How did you let your boss know about this idea?
- ◆   What did your boss say about the idea?
- ◆   Tell me how you implemented your idea.
- ◆   How often in the past 6 months have you shown this kind of initiative?
- ◆   Tell me about the most recent one. [repeat probes]

6.3   Another aspect of supervisory positions is to inform other cashiers of changes in rules and regulations. Think of the most recent time when you had to inform other people of a change in procedures.

- ◆   What was the change?
- ◆   How did you inform the people involved?
- ◆   Did you receive any comments about your way of doing it?
- ◆   How often have you performed this kind of task?
- ◆   Did you have to correct someone who didn't quite get it? What were they doing wrong? How did you correct it?

0.5   My last set of questions deals with your people skills. Let's start by having you sum up your skills in dealing with people.

2.1   I would like to narrow that in a bit to an example of a time when you effectively used your people skills to solve a customer problem.

- ◆   When did this take place?
- ◆   What did the customer say?
- ◆   What did you say in response?
- ◆   How did the customer react? Was the customer satisfied?

2.3   Now think of the most frustrating time you have experienced when trying to help solve a customer problem.

- What led up to this event?
- What did the customer want?
- How did you first respond to the customer?
- What made this incident so frustrating?
- In the end, what did the customer do?
- Did your boss say anything about this event? What?
- Did this type of problem occur at other times?
- How did you handle it then?
- What steps did you take to avoid this type of problem?

2.4 As a supervisor, you will sometimes have to settle disagreements among cashiers. Tell me about the biggest disagreement among cashiers you helped resolve.

- What was the disagreement about?
- When did you first notice it?
- What did you first do to help settle it?
- What did you say?
- How did the disagreeing parties respond to your idea?
- How was the argument eventually settled?
- How often have you helped in this type of situation?

♦ Computer Programmer

♦ BEHAVIOR DIMENSIONS

1. Demonstrates technical expertise in writing programs, applying the full power of the software and hardware *versus* is sloppy and careless in writing programs, taking many more operations than necessary.
2. Checks work and tests programs in a meticulous and thorough manner *versus* overlooks errors, doesn't thoroughly debug and verify test programs.
3. Organizes and manages workload in accordance with schedule constraints, keeps supervisor informed of project progress *versus* is disorganized, constantly misses deadlines, fails to give up-to-date progress reports, tries to handle problems alone.
4. Demonstrates the ability to extract what the user really needs, provides advice and assistance to users when necessary *versus* has little or no communication with users.
5. Writes complete, concise, and understandable documentation for all programs *versus* documents in a confusing, incomplete manner.
6. Demonstrates a willingness to learn new procedures, keeps up to date with recent technological developments *versus* sticks to routine ways of doing things, is out of touch with progress in the field.
7. Contributes to pleasant, cooperative, and professional relations with staff *versus* argues, bickers, and causes resentment and dissension.
8. Works steadily and conscientiously *versus* wastes time.

◆ INTERVIEW QUESTIONS

Recent Work Experience

0.1   I would like to start by having you briefly describe your duties and responsibilities in your most recent position.

Related Work Habits

8.1   Every job has its busy and slow periods. Tell me about the busiest time you faced on your last job.

- ◆   When did this happen?
- ◆   What did you do to prepare yourself for this period?
- ◆   How did you know what to expect?
- ◆   How did your preparations help you handle this period?
- ◆   What comments, if any, did your supervisor make about your ability to handle a rush?

8.2   Now I would like you to tell me about the most recent slack time that you faced.

- ◆   When did this happen?
- ◆   How slow was this period compared to your normal workload?
- ◆   What were your co-workers doing at this time?
- ◆   Did you request other work during this period?
- ◆   [If yes] Tell me about a time when you requested other work.

1.1   We all like to be recognized for doing a job well. Tell me about the last time you were complimented on one of your projects.

- ◆   What was the project?
- ◆   Who gave you the compliment?
- ◆   What did that person say?
- ◆   Who designed the project?
- ◆   How did you come to be assigned the project?
- ◆   Who else was involved in the project?
- ◆   What was your responsibility with regard to the project?
- ◆   What was it about the project that led to the compliment?
- ◆   How often do you receive such compliments on your work in a 6-month period?

7.1 Tell me about the most undesirable project you were assigned.

- ♦ What was the project?
- ♦ What was it about the project that made it undesirable?
- ♦ How did you go about completing the project?
- ♦ How long did it take you?
- ♦ Was the project completed within the budget assigned to it?
- ♦ How did you check out the quality of your work on this project?

2.1 Sometimes, if we're not careful, we can overlook an error. Tell me about a time that you avoided making a mistake as a result of rechecking a program.

- ♦ What was the particular program involved?
- ♦ What steps did you go through in rechecking the program?
- ♦ How did you find the mistake?
- ♦ What problems were avoided as a result of finding the error immediately?
- ♦ How often do you find yourself in this situation?

2.2 Unfortunately, we don't always manage to catch mistakes. Can you recall a mistake that you missed that was most embarrassing for you?

- ♦ What was the mistake?
- ♦ How was the mistake brought to your attention?
- ♦ How did the error get through your detection methods?
- ♦ What problems developed as a result of the mistake?
- ♦ What action did you take to avoid this type of mistake in the future?
- ♦ Were you able to catch this type of mistake the next time it occurred?

1.2 Describe for me the program you wrote that you consider to be your personal best.

- ♦ What was the program?
- ♦ Why do you feel that it was your best?
- ♦ What parts of the program were the most satisfying?
- ♦ How was the way you wrote this program different from the way you normally write one?

♦ What comments, if any, did your supervisor make about the program?

0.2   I'd like to concentrate now on how you organize and manage your projects. What skills do you possess in this area?

3.1   One way to organize the completion of a program on time is to set personal goals to complete various parts of the program. Tell me about a time when setting such goals helped you complete a program on time.

♦ What was the program?
♦ How did you organize the various parts of the program to be done?
♦ How did you set your goals for this task?
♦ How did you keep track of your goal accomplishment?
♦ How often do you organize a task in this way?

3.2   Everyone always needs their programs "right now." Tell me about a time when you had a lot of programs to write and very little time to do them in.

♦ When did this happen?
♦ How did you manage to complete each program on time?
♦ How did you allocate your time to the various programs?
♦ How much overtime was necessary to complete everything on time?
♦ How often do you find yourself in this type of situation over a period of 6 months?

3.3   Tell me about one of your projects that fell most seriously behind schedule.

♦ What was the project?
♦ What were the major obstacles that you encountered?
♦ How did you attempt to overcome these obstacles?
♦ What was the outcome of your efforts?
♦ What effect did the delay have for the person requesting the program?
♦ What steps did you take to avoid future delays of this type?
♦ How often did projects fall behind schedule last year?

3.4   Describe for me a time when you neglected to keep your supervisor up to date on the progress of a particular project and as a result caused a serious problem.

- What was the project?
- What were the circumstances that led up to the incident?
- How did you become aware of the problem?
- How did the lack of information on progress lead to the problem?
- What steps did you take to correct the situation?
- What did your supervisor say regarding the matter?

User Interpersonal Skills

0.3   One of the most important relationships we must develop is that between ourselves and the user. What strengths do you have in this area?

4.1   Sometimes users come to us for a program and they aren't really sure what they want. Tell me about a time when you were able to help a user define his or her needs and then delivered a program that fit those needs.

- What was the user not clear about?
- What did you do to help the user come up with some concrete needs?
- What was the user's reaction to your efforts?
- How did the way you handled this situation differ from the way you normally handle such situations?
- How often does this kind of problem come up in a 6-month period?

4.2   Tell me about the most frustrating time you have experienced when trying to help solve a user's problem.

- What led up to the situation?
- What did the user want?
- How did you initially respond to the user?
- What was it about the situation that you found so frustrating?
- How did the situation end?
- What comments, if any, did your supervisor make about the situation?
- What did you do the next time this type of situation arose?

4.3 Can you recall a specific instance when you did something for a user that was more than the job required?

- ♦ When did this happen?
- ♦ What did you do for the user that was beyond the requirements?
- ♦ What were your reasons for taking this action?
- ♦ What was the user's reaction?
- ♦ What did he or she say to you?
- ♦ How did this extra work fit in with your regular workload?
- ♦ How often do you do a little extra work?

Documentation Skills

0.4 This next set of questions deals with documentation. What do you feel are the key factors involved in doing good documentation?

5.1 Working with a program written by someone who didn't produce understandable documentation can be very frustrating. Tell me about a time when you were in this type of situation.

- ♦ What sort of work were you doing?
- ♦ What was it about the documentation that made it confusing?
- ♦ How did you handle the problem?
- ♦ What was the outcome?
- ♦ What steps did you take to improve the documentation so that it could be more easily understood for future programmers?
- ♦ How often do you come across poor documentation over a 6-month period?

5.2 Can you recall a specific time where your documentation helped a fellow worker with his job?

- ♦ What was it about your documentation that was helpful?
- ♦ What did your co-workers say to you about your documentation?
- ♦ How many times in the past year has your documentation been helpful to others?

5.3   Please explain to me how you documented your most recently completed project.

- When did you complete the documentation for each part of the assignment?
- What parts of the documentation were the most essential?
- How long did it take you?
- How did it differ from the way you usually document?
- What comments, if any, have you received on your documentation?

5.4   Tell me about a time when, because of time constraints, you did not document as well as you would have liked.

- What circumstances led up to the situation?
- What parts of the documentation were you the least satisfied with?
- How was the usefulness of the program affected by the poor documentation?
- How did you remedy the situation?
- What steps did you take to avoid this type of situation in the future?

5.5   Can you recall the last time your supervisor asked to recheck your documentation?

- What reasons did he or she give for wanting to recheck it?
- What were the results of the rechecking?
- What comments did he or she make?
- As a result, what steps have you taken to change your method of documentation?

Job-Related Experiences

0.5   I would like to switch topics now and focus on how you keep up to date on your profession. Describe briefly how you keep up with recent technological developments in the field.

6.1   Can you think of some work you completed recently that best reflects how you apply new techniques to solve practical problems?

- What was the problem?
- What new technique did you use?
- How did you learn of this technique?
- What was the outcome associated with using the technique?
- How was the technique better or worse than the techniques you normally use?
- What comments, if any, did your supervisor have?

6.2 Most companies give in-house seminars or presentations to help further our knowledge. Tell me about the last in-house training session you attended.

- What was the session about?
- What did you learn?
- How has this information helped you in your job?
- How useful was it in comparison to other such sessions that you have attended?
- How did you communicate what you had learned to your co-workers?

Co-Worker Interpersonal Skills

0.6 I would like to finish up by focusing some questions on your relationships with your supervisor and co-workers. Could you outline for me what you think your interpersonal strengths are?

7.1 It is often necessary to work together in a group to accomplish a task. Can you tell me about the most recent experience you had working as part of a group?

- What was the task?
- How many people were in the group?
- What difficulties arose as a result of working as a group?
- What role did you play in resolving these difficulties?
- How successful was the group in completing the task?
- How often do you work as part of a group?

7.2 At one time or another, everyone has become upset over a task assigned by the supervisor. Tell me about the last time this happened to you.

♦ What was the task?
♦ How did you come to be assigned to the task?
♦ What was it about the task that upset you?
♦ How did you let your supervisor know that you were upset?
♦ How did he or she respond to you?
♦ How was the situation eventually smoothed out?
♦ How often do you react this way to assignments?

7.3 Tell me about a time when you were able to help a co-worker through a difficult situation.

♦ What led up to the situation?
♦ How did you become involved?
♦ How were you able to help?
♦ What reaction did your co-worker have to your attempts to help?
♦ How often do you find yourself in this type of situation?

7.4 We often become involved in disputes between people in other departments. Can you recall a specific time when this happened?

♦ What was the problem?
♦ How did you happen to be involved?
♦ How was the dispute resolved?
♦ How satisfied were the members of both departments with the solution?
♦ What effect did the situation have on your future relations with the members of that department?

7.5 When a new person comes into the job, we are often given the responsibility of training that person. Tell me about the most recent time you experienced a personality conflict with someone you were training.

♦ What was it about the other person that you had difficulty dealing with?
♦ How did you attempt to overcome your differences?
♦ What was the other person's reaction to your attempts?
♦ How did this tension affect your training experience?
♦ What was the outcome?
♦ What is your relationship with that person today?

♦   What comments did your supervisor make about the way you handled the situation?

7.6   Tell me about the most favorable comment you have received from a member of the staff.

♦   What did the person say?
♦   What led up to the incident?
♦   What impact did this comment have on your behavior?
♦   How often did you receive such comments?

♦ Computer Science Engineer

♦ BEHAVIOR DIMENSIONS

1. Debates or verifies important data *versus* assumes important data are correct without rechecking.
2. Keeps up to date with internal and external research in job-related topics *versus* is out of touch with recent research.
3. Follows *versus* ignores company policies and standards.
4. Works steadily and conscientiously *versus* wastes time.
5. Meets *versus* misses schedule and budget commitments.
6. Documents software clearly and completely *versus* produces software that is difficult for others to follow.
7. Seeks stretching assignments, is creative *versus* avoids challenge, prefers the routine.
8. Relates pleasantly and professionally to peers and supervisors *versus* argues and bickers with those who have different views.

♦ INTERVIEW QUESTIONS

Recent Work Experience

0.1 Describe briefly your duties and responsibilities in your most recent position.

7.1 Tell me about the last time you were complimented on your project work.

- ♦ Who gave you the compliment?
- ♦ What did that person say?

141

- Who designed the project? Who assigned it?
- Who besides you worked on this project?
- What were their roles?
- What did you do that led to the compliment?
- How many compliments did you receive last year?
- Tell me about the one that gives you the greatest sense of accomplishment. [repeat probes]

6.1 Staying with your recent work experience, please explain how you documented your most recently completed project. Start with the initial design and take me through handing the finished product over for operation.

- When did you complete the documentation for each phase of the project?
- Did you ever receive any comments about your documentation?
- What were the comments?

6.2 Explaining documentation to operations people or to peers is sometimes frustrating. Tell me about the most frustrating time you have had explaining your documentation to someone else.

- What was it that they did not seem to pick up?
- How did you eventually get your message across?
- What steps did you take to avoid this kind of difficulty?
- How often has this kind of problem come up?

3.1 In large organizations, following organizational policy is important. Can you think of a time when you followed a company policy with which you didn't agree 100 percent?

- What was the company policy?
- What did you find objectionable about the policy?
- What was the outcome of following the policy?
- How often did you find yourself in this type of situation?
- What steps did you take to change this policy?

3.2 Tell me about an organizational policy you had some role in changing.

- [Same probes as 3.1]

2.1 It is often difficult to keep track of all the new technical developments. Can you think of some work you completed recently that best reflects how you apply new techniques to solve practical problems?

♦ What was the problem?
♦ What was the new technique and how did you learn of it?
♦ How did your solution work out in practice?
♦ Did your boss comment on this work? What was said?

2.2 Tell me about the meeting or presentation within the past 6 months that you feel was most worthwhile.

♦ What was the meeting about?
♦ When was it held?
♦ Did you take any notes? How many pages?
♦ Did you ask any questions? Can you recall them?
♦ How did you communicate what you learned to your boss? To others?

Research Experience

0.2 I would like to switch topics from past job-related experience to focus on your research experience. Please outline your research strengths.

2.3 One task facing CS engineers is presenting research findings to peers. Tell me about your most successful research presentation.

♦ What was the topic of the presentation?
♦ How did you structure your material?
♦ How long did you take to prepare for this presentation?
♦ How many people attended the presentation?
♦ Did you receive any comments about the presentation?
♦ Was the presentation evaluated formally in any way?
♦ How many research presentations did you give last year?

2.4 Sometimes we have all had a research presentation fall flat. Tell me about the most frustrating presentation you made last year.

♦ What was the topic of the presentation?
♦ What obstacle led to the frustration?
♦ How did you try to overcome the obstacle?

♦ What was the result of your efforts?
♦ What steps did you take to try to avoid this type of problem in the future?
♦ Were they successful? Tell me about a time when they were.
♦ How often has this type of situation come up in the past year?

1.1   Tell me about the last time you avoided making a mistake as a result of rechecking a program or system.

♦ What was the system or program concerned?
♦ What was the mistake you avoided?
♦ How serious were the consequences of that mistake?
♦ How often has this type of situation come up?
♦ Tell me about another one. [repeat probes]

1.2   Everyone always has a story about "the one that got away." Tell me about the mistake you missed that was most embarrassing for you.

♦ What was the mistake?
♦ How had you tried to check for this type of error?
♦ How did this error get through your detection efforts?
♦ What were the consequences of this mistake?
♦ What steps did you take to avoid this in the future?
♦ Were you able to detect this type of mistake the next time it occurred? When was that?

2.5   Can you recall a project in which your research skill enabled you to find the right solution, not just the obvious one?

♦ Please describe the project goals and objectives.
♦ What was your role in the project?
♦ How did you apply knowledge from research to this problem?
♦ What were the consequences of taking the obvious solution?
♦ How often has this type of situation come up in the past year?

7.2   Keeping up with technical reading is quite a chore. Try leading me through a brief description of the technical reading you have done in the past month.

♦ When did you fit your technical reading in?
♦ Is this past month typical? Which recent month is more typical? What did you read in that month?

7.3 Tell me about your most innovative project.

♦ Who assigned the project and when?
♦ How did you assess user needs on this project?
♦ Who worked on the project and what did they contribute?
♦ What did you do that was innovative?
♦ What were the payoffs for the organization?
♦ How often did you make this kind of innovation contribution?

4.1 Returning for a moment to research presentations, there are always some presentations for which a person is better prepared than others. Think of a time when you were most frustrated by short deadlines that led to your being disappointed in your preparation for a presentation or meeting.

♦ When did this occur?
♦ How many people attended the presentation?
♦ What were the consequences for the group of your lack of preparation?
♦ What steps did you take to overcome this type of problem?
♦ How effective were those steps? Tell me about a time when they were effective (ineffective).

Budgeting, Planning, and Scheduling Experiences

0.3 Turning to another major area of the job, the next few questions look at budgeting, planning, and scheduling. How do you typically go about planning a budget?

5.1 Tell me about your most recent project that came in on time and within budget.

♦ When was this project completed?
♦ What was your involvement in the budget for this project?
♦ How did you go about deciding on the budget?

- How did you draw up the schedule?
- What were the key factors in meeting the schedule?
- What percentage of projects you designed came in this way?

5.2   Everyone has projects that fall behind for one reason or another. Tell me about one of your projects that fell most seriously behind schedule.

- When did this project occur?
- What was your role in drawing up the schedule?
- What were the major obstacles that held up the project?
- What steps did you take to overcome these obstacles?
- What was the outcome of those steps?
- How did you tackle this kind of situation the next time it came up? When was that? What happened?
- How often did projects fall behind schedule last year?

4.2   One way to avoid over-budget and behind-deadline projects is to set personal goals to complete various phases of a project. Tell me about the project in which setting several goals helped the most toward bringing in the project on time.

- What were the objectives of the project?
- How did you go about breaking the project down into tasks?
- How did you set goals for those tasks?
- How did you keep track of your goal accomplishment?
- How many projects did you handle this way?

7.4   Tell me about the last time that you worked overtime to meet a project deadline.

- Did the project meet the deadline?
- What factors made the overtime necessary?
- How often has overtime been needed in the past 6 months?

5.3   Just as some projects get behind schedule, some also go over budget. I would like to hear about the project that most frustrated you on budget overrun.

- When did this project occur?
- What were the circumstances that led to the overrun?

+ What steps did you take to keep the lid on?
+ What did you learn from this experience?
+ How did you handle the next project that started going over budget?
+ What percentage of your projects went over budget?

Communication Experience

0.4 The next few questions assess how effectively you get your ideas across to others. Maybe we could start by having you state a couple of your communications strengths.

8.1 Now I would like to focus in on a recent time when you used one of those strengths to help resolve a misunderstanding between you and one of your co-workers.

+ What was the subject of the misunderstanding?
+ How did you put your view on the first go-around?
+ What did the other person say in response?
+ How did you try to clarify the situation?
+ How did you know that the other person eventually got the message?
+ How often have situations like this come up in the past 6 months?

8.2 It's impossible to please someone all the time. Tell me about the most serious disagreement you had with your supervisor over some aspect of your work.

+ When did this happen?
+ What led to the disagreement?
+ How did your supervisor first bring up the topic?
+ What did you say in response?
+ What was the outcome of the disagreement?
+ Did you decide to handle this kind of situation differently after that?
+ [If so] How did you handle it the next time it came up?

8.3 Sooner or later, everyone gets caught up in memo writing. Please tell me about your greatest success in drafting a memo that got the message across.

♦ What was the subject of the memo?
♦ To whom was it addressed?
♦ How long was the memo? How long did it take you to write it?
♦ Did you perform any editing before sending it out?
♦ How much did you change?
♦ How do you know that the message was clearly received?
♦ How many memos have you written in the past month?

8.4 Memos often are a difficult medium. Tell me about the most frustrating time you have had as a result of someone misunderstanding one of your memos.

♦ What was the memo trying to get across?
♦ What was misread in the memo?
♦ How could you have gotten it across more clearly?
♦ How often has this type of situation come up in the past 6 months?

Leadership Experience

0.4 In your view, how does leadership fit into the role of computer science engineer.

7.5 Tell me about the most recent time you demonstrated leadership on the job.

♦ What was the background to this event?
♦ When did this happen?
♦ What did you do that influenced others?
♦ What was the reaction to your leadership?
♦ How often did this type of situation arise in the past year?

7.6 Tell me about the time when you were most successful in leading a group toward accomplishing an important goal.

♦ When did this happen?
♦ What was the goal? Who defined the goal?
♦ How were the steps leading to the goal defined?
♦ What was your role in implementing those steps?
♦ Did you receive comments from your boss about this event?

♦ What was said? What about comments from peers, subordinates?

3.3 Sometimes, people are called on to make decisions when their immediate supervisor is away. Tell me about the most important decision you were asked to make when your boss was away.

♦ What was the decision about?
♦ Why was the boss absent at the time? For how long?
♦ How did you go about making the decision?
♦ What were the alternatives that you considered?
♦ What were your boss's comments when he or she returned?

3.4 Another type of situation occurs when it becomes necessary to skirt around guidelines to accomplish an important goal. All companies have set procedures and guidelines, and sometimes these get in the way of completing a project. Tell me about the last time you had to move around some guidelines, perhaps because you had a more efficient method.

♦ What were the guidelines that got in the way?
♦ What did you want to do that conflicted with them?
♦ How did you size up the possible outcomes before acting?
♦ What was the outcome of your action?
♦ Did your boss make any comments about this? Did your boss know?
♦ How often did this type of situation arise in the past year?
♦ Have you ever handled this type of situation differently? How so?

7.7 Changing the subject again, can you think of a specific incident when you did something for a user that was "beyond the call of duty"?

♦ When did this happen?
♦ What were your reasons for taking this action?
♦ How did the user react? What was said?
♦ How did this fit in with your other assignments at the time?
♦ Did your boss comment on this extra work?

7.8   On the same theme, can you think back to the last time you were asked to help out on a project that you weren't directly assigned to?

- When did this happen?
- What project were you asked to help with?
- What was your workload like at the time?
- What were you asked to do? How long would it take?
- What did you do? How successful was your assistance?
- How often did this type of situation arise in the past year?

7.9   We are all asked to take additional responsibilities or assignments that we just can't fit in. Tell me about the last time you were unable to accept some additional work.

- When did this happen?
- What were you asked to do? By whom?
- What was your workload at the time?
- Why did you feel you could not accept this request?
- How often did this type of situation arise in the past year?

4.3   Please tell me about the most undesirable assignment you were handed last year.

- What was the assignment? What made it undesirable?
- Who gave you the assignment?
- How did you go about completing the assignment?
- Was the assignment completed on schedule? On budget?
- How did you check out the quality of your work on this assignment?

♦ Government Laborer

♦ BEHAVIOR DIMENSIONS

1. Uses and maintains equipment carefully *versus* abuses equipment, ignores maintenance.
2. Maintains positive, friendly public relations *versus* insults or provokes members of the public.
3. Gets along smoothly with co-workers *versus* bickers or angers co-workers.
4. Works steadily *versus* wastes time.
5. Completes tasks that meet requirements *versus* turns in products or services that need reworking or patching up.
6. Makes suggestions, makes decisions when needed *versus* waits for direction on minor tasks, merely puts in time.

♦ INTERVIEW QUESTIONS

Previous Work Experience

0.1   I would like to begin by having you tell me a little more about what you did on your most recent job.

1.1   One aspect of your experience that interests us is your experience with machinery. Please list the machines you have used.

1.2   We all know of situations in which using the right machine saves a lot of time. Tell me about a time when you made the best use of machines.

♦   When did this happen?
♦   What was the task?

151

- ♦ What machine did you choose?
- ♦ What machine is normally used for that task?
- ♦ How much time and effort was saved?
- ♦ What was your part in choosing this machine?
- ♦ Do you have another story like this one? What is it?

1.3 Machines eventually break down. Tell me about the time that an equipment breakdown was most frustrating to you.

- ♦ What was the equipment?
- ♦ What broke down on the equipment?
- ♦ Who was responsible for maintaining that equipment?
- ♦ How was the breakdown handled?
- ♦ What could you have done to prevent this breakdown?
- ♦ What steps did you take to prevent another breakdown?
- ♦ When did the next breakdown occur on this equipment?
- ♦ How often did situations like this come up in the past year?

1.4 Some maintenance procedures are more helpful than others. Tell me about a procedure you used that you figure saved the most headaches later on. When was the last time you applied this procedure?

- ♦ What was the equipment?
- ♦ What was different about your procedure?
- ♦ What kinds of headaches did this procedure avoid?
- ♦ How did you know that this procedure worked?
- ♦ Did you have better procedures for other machines?
- ♦ Tell me about another one.

6.1 I think we have use of equipment tied up, so let's move on. Sometimes your supervisor is not around the worksite but a decision has to be made to complete a task. Tell me about the most important decision you had to make under these circumstances.

- ♦ What was the decision about?
- ♦ Why did your supervisor have to leave?
- ♦ When was the supervisor due back?
- ♦ What action did you decide to take?
- ♦ What was the outcome of this action?
- ♦ What did your boss say upon his or her return?

♦ How often did this type of situation come up in the past year?

6.2 What was the best idea you had for improving the way things were done on your last job?

♦ What were the benefits of your idea?
♦ How did you approach your boss with this idea?
♦ Have other people used this idea since then?
♦ How many ideas like that have you mentioned in the past year?
♦ Tell me about the most recent one.

6.3 Sometimes it is necessary to check with your supervisor before going ahead on a simple task. Tell me about the most recent time that happened to you.

♦ When did this occur?
♦ What was the task?
♦ How did you approach your supervisor: What did he or she say?
♦ How could it have been handled if the boss was away?
♦ How often did this type of situation come up last month?

4.1 Sometimes, during a rush period, people have to miss their breaks just to get the work done. Tell me about the last time that happened to you.

♦ When did this happen?
♦ What was the cause of all the work?
♦ How did you decide to skip your break?
♦ Did anyone else do the same thing?
♦ How often did this situation come up in the past 6 months?

4.2 Just as there are busy times, things also slack off sometimes. Tell me about the quietest day you had in the past year.

♦ When did this happen?
♦ What did you do on that day?
♦ What were the other people doing during that time?
♦ Did your boss make any comments about your efforts?
♦ How often has this situation come up in the past year?

4.3 Switching focus a bit, tell me about a time when you really had to hustle to make it to work on time.

- ♦ When did this happen?
- ♦ What led to your getting pinched for time?
- ♦ Did you actually make it on time?
- ♦ What did you do to avoid this problem in the future?
- ♦ How did you actually handle the next time this came up?

4.4 Every now and then, we all miss a day. Tell me about the most recent day you missed.

- ♦ When did this occur?
- ♦ What caused you to miss the day?
- ♦ When did your boss first learn that you would not be coming in?
- ♦ Did that cause any problems at work?
- ♦ How often have you had to miss a day in the past 6 months?

Interpersonal Relations

0.2 Let's move on to the way you get along with co-workers and the public. First, how do you get along with fellow workers?

3.1 Tell me about the most serious disagreement between two fellow workers that you helped resolve.

- ♦ What was the source of the disagreement?
- ♦ How did you know that it was serious?
- ♦ When did you decide to try to help out?
- ♦ What did you first say in trying to settle things down?
- ♦ How did the workers respond?
- ♦ What was the outcome of your efforts?

3.2 Even people who are reasonable often have disagreements. Tell me about the most heated disagreement you experienced in the past year.

- ♦ When did this event take place?
- ♦ Who was involved?
- ♦ How did the disagreement surface?

♦ What contributed to the argument being heated?
♦ How was the disagreement ended? What was the out-come?
♦ How often did this kind of situation come up in the past year?

3.3 People work at different speeds. Tell me about the most difficult moment you faced with the slowest partner you worked with.

♦ What were the circumstances of this moment?
♦ How did you handle the difference in speed of work?
♦ What did you say to this worker to let your feelings be known?
♦ What was the outcome of all of this?

2.1 Tell me about the most favorable comment you received from a member of the public.

♦ What did the person say?
♦ What led to this event?
♦ What impact did this event have on your behavior?
♦ How often did you receive this type of comment?
♦ Tell me about another one.

2.2 Sometimes, members of the public can be very frustrating. Tell me about the most frustrating time you faced with a member of the public.

♦ What did the person do that frustrated you?
♦ How did you approach the situation?
♦ What did you say to get your point across?
♦ What was the person's response?
♦ How did this situation end up?
♦ How often did this type of situation come up in the past year?

◆ Life Insurance Administrative Consultant

◆ BEHAVIOR DIMENSIONS

1. Detects deficiencies in data or systems *versus* lacks sufficient expertise to detect deficiencies.
2. Works steadily *versus* wastes time.
3. Arranges tasks systematically, follows up details *versus* misplaces files, forgets details, waits until tasks are almost due before working on them.
4. Listens actively, asks questions judiciously to clarify the other person's message *versus* responds defensively to frustrated customers, assumes understanding before it is obtained.
5. Attentively notes important events, informing others *versus* lets important dates or events slip by.

◆ INTERVIEW QUESTIONS

Consultant Experience

0.1 Let's get started by having you tell me about your duties and responsibilities on your most recent job as an administrative consultant. [or job closest to administrative consultant]

1.1 Now I'd like you to think back to your best project on that job—the project you were most proud of.

- ◆ How was this project outstanding in your view?
- ◆ How was the project originated?
- ◆ Who designed the project and assigned people to it?

156

- ♦ Who worked with you on this project?
- ♦ Did you get any feedback from your boss on this project? What was said?

1.2 As I'm sure you know, one kind of situation in which we look for help occurs when an administrative consultant sniffs out some fishy data or is able to tell that a procedure has administrative problems. Can you tell me about the most costly problem or weakness you detected on your last job?

- ♦ What did you do that led you to find the problem?
- ♦ What steps did you take to overcome the problem?
- ♦ What were the savings for the organization?
- ♦ Did you ever notice the same kind of problem cropping up again?
- ♦ What steps did you take to prevent a recurring problem?

3.1 Now I'd like you to think of another project. This time, find the project that gave you the most difficulty. We all have projects that turn into headaches. Tell me about your biggest headache.

- ♦ How did the project get started?
- ♦ What was the obstacle that got in the way?
- ♦ What did you do to try to overcome this obstacle?
- ♦ How did the project eventually turn out?
- ♦ How often did this kind of problem come up in the past year?

2.1 Another situation that sometimes crops up concerns times when things slow down a bit. Tell me about the slowest period on your last job.

- ♦ Was the slowdown seasonal or related to customer demand?
- ♦ What did you do to make most productive use of the time?
- ♦ What were the other administrative consultants doing during this time?
- ♦ Did your boss comment on your effort during this period? What was said?

3.2 One way to give me a good picture of the way you handle your job is for you to lead me through a specific day. What was your most recent complete working day on your last job? Let's just walk through the day from the time you arrived in the morning.

- ♦ What was the first thing you did that day?
- ♦ That takes us up to [time]. What did you do next?
- ♦ Do you remember what you actually said?
- ♦ What did he or she say in reply?
- ♦ How long did that take?

5.1 It's often been said that the administrative consultant's job is to fight fires. What was the biggest fire you put out on your last job?

- ♦ What was the fire about?
- ♦ What steps did you take to resolve the problem?
- ♦ How did the problem come up in the first place?
- ♦ What steps did you take to make sure it didn't happen again?
- ♦ Did it ever happen again? How often?
- ♦ Thinking back, what could you have done to prevent it?
- ♦ Did your boss say anything? What?

5.2 Sometimes an administrative consultant can save everyone a lot of time just by noticing an important upcoming event and letting others know about it. Tell me about the last time you did this.

- ♦ How did you notice the event?
- ♦ What did you do to make sure others took note of it?

Interpersonal Experiences

0.2 Could you outline for me what you think your interpersonal strengths are?

4.1 As an administrative consultant with us, you will sometimes find yourself dealing with irate customers or staff. Can you locate a time when you used your interpersonal strengths to effectively resolve a problem with an irate person?

- ♦ What specifically was the problem?
- ♦ How did you find out what the problem was?
- ♦ What did the person say? How did you know the person was upset or angry?

◆ How was the problem resolved in the end?
◆ How satisfied was the person with the solution?
◆ How were you able to tell how satisfied the person was?
◆ Did you ever hear anything more about this incident? What?

2.2 No matter where you work, a friend will sometimes come up to "chit-chat" when you have work to do. Tell me about the last time this happened to you.

◆ What did you say to the friend?
◆ What did the friend do?
◆ When was the next time you talked to that person?

4.2 Sometimes, explaining a new idea or a difficult concept to someone is very frustrating because the person just doesn't seem to get it. Tell me about the most frustrating time you had explaining a new company policy or a complex idea to someone.

◆ What was the idea you were trying to explain?
◆ What seemed to be the problem with getting the idea across?
◆ What approaches did you try to get the idea to sink in?
◆ How could you tell if you were being successful?
◆ What did you say after you saw you weren't getting very far?
◆ How often has this kind of problem come up in the past year?

4.3 Is there some activity outside of work in which you used your interpersonal skills to good advantage?

◆ What were your tasks in this activity?
◆ Can you give a specific example of using a strength?
◆ What did you do that helped solve a problem?
◆ How often were you called upon in this way in the past year?

♦ Middle Manager (Petroleum)

♦ BEHAVIOR DIMENSIONS

1. Takes action to achieve objectives, maintains a sense of urgency, seeks out opportunities for the company *versus* waits to be told what to do, reacts to developing crises.
2. Supports decisions with logical arguments from the perspective of corporate need *versus* makes snap decisions based on personal considerations or inadequate evidence.
3. Thoroughly prepares in advance for meetings and presentations, drawing on files and personal contacts, organizes team member tasks in a logical sequence, drawing on team members' skills, recognizes approaching bottlenecks, mobilizing the required resources in advance *versus* is unprepared for peak period activity, requiring extensive overtime authorization, assigns tasks to inappropriate team members or in confusing sequences, "wings it" in presentations, passing over important issues.
4. Communicates specific time and resource objectives when delegating tasks, provides regular feedback on task accomplishment, rewards effective work with positive feedback, clarifies authority and responsibility of team members, demonstrates concern for the fair treatment of all team members *versus* provides vague, general directions on desirable results that include few specifics, allows authority levels to emerge among team members, notices and criticizes only poor performance, is concerned solely with visible results.
5. Maintains awareness of developing interpersonal conflicts, deals directly with conflicts by constructively confronting the issues, acts as a mediator when conflicts interfere with working relationships *versus* suppresses or ignores conflict, waiting for it to go away, avoids team conflicts by assigning others to resolve them.

160

6. Maintains a network of personal contacts within the company and industry to keep up to date with new opportunities, to remain aware of recent solutions to common problems, and to be fully prepared when negotiating for the company *versus* sticks to established friendships based on social compatability, avoids opportunities to develop new contacts.

♦ INTERVIEW QUESTIONS

0.1 Let's begin by having you review your duties and responsibilities on your most recent job.

1.1 Thinking back on that job, pick out your finest hour; that is, describe the assignment or project that you feel best demonstrated your management skills.
   ♦ Where did the idea for this assignment or project originate?
   ♦ What was your role in developing the project concept?
   ♦ What did you do to promote the concept within the company?
   ♦ How did you keep the project moving as things progressed?

2.1 Staying with that project, how did you decide that this project or assignment had merit?
   ♦ What kinds of arguments persuaded you to support the project?
   ♦ What arguments did you develop yourself when supporting this project with your peers and superiors?
   ♦ How successful was the project? How did you reach your conclusions?

1.2 As managers, we have all been called on at one time or another to revive a project or assignment that was losing steam. Tell me about the last time you had to create a sense of urgency to get a team or an individual motivated again.

♦ What was the project or assignment?
♦ Who assigned the project in the first place?
♦ How did it become bogged down?
♦ What did you do to motivate the involvement of team members?
♦ Were your efforts successful? How did you know?
♦ Did the project reach its objectives? What comments were made?
♦ How often did this type of situation come up in the past year?

3.2 Meetings and presentations are an important part of a manager's job. Tell me about your most successful presentation to a management meeting.

♦ What was the topic of your presentation?
♦ What were your objectives for the meeting?
♦ When did you start preparing for the meeting? What did you do?
♦ How were those preparations useful during the meeting?
♦ What was decided at the meeting? What were the long-term outcomes?
♦ Did anyone comment on your presentation? What was said?
♦ What percentage of the time did your meetings go like this one?

3.3 We can all recall a time when we had to make a presentation or attend a meeting on short notice when we weren't very well prepared. Tell me about the presentation or meeting you would most like to forget.

♦ When did you first learn about the meeting or presentation?
♦ [Same probes as for 3.2]

6.1 Maintaining a network of personal contacts helps a manager keep on top of developments. Describe some of your most useful personal contacts.

♦ Tell me about a time when a personal contact helped you solve a problem or avoid a major blunder.
♦ How did you develop that contact in the first place?

♦ What did you do to obtain the useful information from your contact?
♦ When was the next time this contact was useful? What was the situation at that time?
♦ How often in the past 6 months have personal contacts been useful in this way?

6.2 Given the usefulness of contacts, building new contacts pays off. Focusing on the past 6 months, describe an example of the way you build your contacts.

♦ When did this example take place?
♦ Has this particular contact paid off yet? How?
♦ How often have you used this type of approach to building contacts during the past year?

2.2 We value managers who take a corporate perspective over departmental or personal positions. This may take a minute to find, but tell me about a time when you made your best argument based on corporate need over department or personal advantage.

♦ What were the advantages to the company that you were promoting?
♦ What were the potential costs to your department or yourself?
♦ How did you make your argument?
♦ Were you successful in promoting your view? How do you measure that success?
♦ How often did you make this type of argument? Tell me briefly about the next time this came up.

1.3 Digging up opportunities for our company to improve its current operations or to move into profitable new areas is a key managerial responsibility. Tell me about an opportunity you initiated on your most recent job that produced the biggest payoff for the company.

♦ What specifically was the change you initiated?
♦ When did the idea first come to you?
♦ How did you develop a plan of action from the initial idea?
♦ To whom did you talk in promoting the idea and gaining approval for it?

- Who else helped you out in implementing the idea?
- How successful was this change? How did you measure that success?
- How often were you able to make this kind of contribution?
- Tell me about one other change similar in importance to this one.

0.2   I would like to change our theme now to how you interact with people. Could you begin by sketching out two or three key strengths you have in dealing with people?

- Can you illustrate the first strength with a recent example?
- When did this example take place?
- What possible negative outcomes were avoided by the way you handled this incident?
- How often has this type of situation arisen?
- What happened the next time this came up?
- [Repeat same probes for second strength. Remember to record the dimension number appropriate to the example cited by the applicant.]

4.1   I would like you to take me back to your most recent major project. Try to recall the details of the project meeting with your subordinates when you communicated their objectives for the project. Tell me how you did that.

- When did this meeting take place?
- Can you remember what you said to each team member?
- How did you decide which task to give which team member?
- Did team members receive anything in writing before or after the meeting?
- Did any team members ask questions? Try to recall what they asked. What were your answers?

4.2   Sometimes, in spite of our best effort, subordinates remain confused about their objectives on a project or assignment. Can you tell me about the most recent time this happened to you?

♦ What were the project objectives?
♦ What was the source of the team member's confusion?
♦ How did you find out that the team member was unclear about objectives?
♦ How did you help clarify the situation?
♦ How effective was that team member following your discussion?
♦ How often did you handle situations like this in the past 6 months?

4.3 Letting people know how they are doing is a key managerial responsibility. Let's go back over the last few times you discussed a team member's performance. Perhaps you could start by recalling the most recent time.

♦ What caused you to notice the performance?
♦ What did you say to the team member?
♦ How did the team member respond?
♦ Did you notice any change in performance following your discussion? What?
♦ Now let's back up and look at the time before that. [Repeat probes 2-4 times]

5.1 Handling conflicts between yourself and your subordinates or among your team members is a part of any manager's job. I would like to hear about the most challenging conflict situation you faced and how you handled it.

♦ Who was involved in the conflict?
♦ How did you first learn about it?
♦ What was the source of the conflict?
♦ What did you do to help resolve the conflict?
♦ What was the outcome of this situation?
♦ How often did this type of situation come up in the past year?
♦ Have you ever handled it differently? What happened that time?

5.2 We have all experienced conflicts that turned destructive. Tell me about the most destructive conflict you have experienced.

♦   [Same probes as for 5.1]

5.3   As managers, we are called on to mediate conflicts among team members. Tell me about the conflict you mediated most successfully.

♦   [Same probes as for 5.1]

♦ Nurse

♦ BEHAVIOR DIMENSIONS

1. Establishes and maintains supportive, constructive, and responsive relationships with co-workers *versus* demonstrates insensitivity and lack of cooperation with regard to peer relationships.
2. Manages time effectively, sets priorities, and works steadily *versus* takes unnecessary breaks, avoids, procrastinates, or complains about unpleasant tasks.
3. Processes and charts information and orders carefully in a clear, concise, legible manner *versus* does sloppy processing and irresponsible, unreadable, incomplete charting.
4. Shows compassion and concern for the comfort and well-being of patients and takes the time to develop a rapport with them *versus* remains aloof and distant, treats patients like a "number."
5. Follows nursing and hospital procedures in a proper and professional manner *versus* shows no regard for procedures.

♦ INTERVIEW QUESTIONS

0.1 I'd like to start by having you tell me about your work experience. Start with your most recent position and work backward, briefly detailing your duties and responsibilities.

2.1 The B.Sc.N. program is very demanding academically. Tell me about the most challenging term project you had to prepare.

♦ What was the project?
♦ How did you plan the project and allocate your time?

167

♦ Did you do all of your projects in this manner? If not, how did you handle them?
♦ How long did it take to complete the project?
♦ What comments did your instructor make about the completed project?

5.1 One aspect of any nursing position is to plan patient discharge. Describe a time that you arranged a discharge for a patient who was to receive ongoing health care at home.

♦ What elements of your nursing assessment did you weigh in making your decisions?
♦ What services did you arrange for the patient?
♦ Who did you consult in making these arrangements?
♦ What was the patient's reaction to early discharge, and how did you respond?
♦ What were your supervisor's comments on the arrangements?

4.1 There never seems to be enough staff on duty, especially on the night shift. Tell me about the last night shift you worked that was really hectic.

♦ How did you go about making sure that all of your patients were properly attended to (e.g., medication, dressings changed, etc.)?
♦ How was this shift different from other night shifts that you have worked?
♦ How did you react to the situation?

2.2 When the unit is slack, we sometimes take a little extra time at coffee or lunch. This may happen accidentally because we are not pressed for time. Tell me about a time that you were in a situation like this.

♦ What were the circumstances that caused you to take some extra time?
♦ How often have these types of situations occurred within the past 6 months?
♦ What did you do the next time a situation like this came up?
♦ Did your supervisor make any comments about the extra time?

2.3   All jobs have some unpleasant tasks that are boring or physically uncomfortable. Can you recall the most unpleasant task you were asked to do at work?

♦   What was the task?
♦   Who requested that you do the task?
♦   How often were you asked to do the task?
♦   What was your response to the request?
♦   Did you always respond in this manner? If not, how else have you responded?
♦   Who among your co-workers is asked to do this task most often, and why?

3.1   I'd like to focus now on the more clerical aspects of the position. Because nursing in a hospital is sometimes hectic, a hasty assessment can result in an incomplete or misleading chart. Can you describe the hasty decision that you would most like to do over?

♦   What method was used in charting the assessment S.O.A.P., head-to-toe, etc.)?
♦   Why was the assessment incomplete?
♦   What was the outcome of the incomplete assessment?
♦   How did you become involved in the situation?
♦   What steps were taken to correct the situation, and who took them?
♦   What was your reaction to the situation?
♦   What were the supervisor's comments?

3.2   Describe a time when your charting was useful in making a decision regarding the medical treatment of a patient.

♦   What method did you use in assessing the patient?
♦   What information did you include in that charting?
♦   How did that information help in the decision that was made?
♦   How often did this situation occur within the past 6 months?
♦   Did your supervisor comment on your contribution?
♦   How much of your workday do you normally spend on charting?

3.3   Describe the last time you had to process a doctor's orders with regard to a patient's care.

- What were the orders?
- Do you always do the processing in this way? If not, how else have you done it?
- How long did it take you to process the orders?
- What kind of feedback have you received with regard to your order processing?

0.2   This next set of questions deals with hospital policies and medical procedures. How important do you think it is to have set policies and procedures?

5.2   Tell me about a specific time when you came across a new and unfamiliar procedure.

- What was the procedure?
- What was unfamiliar about it?
- What steps did you take to accomplish the procedure?
- Did you discuss the procedure with your supervisor?
- How did you prepare yourself to handle the procedure the next time it came up?

5.3   Tell me about a time when a doctor wrote an order contrary to hospital policy and asked you to process it.

- How did you bring it to the doctor's attention?
- What did you say to the doctor?
- What was the doctor's reaction?
- How did the order eventually get processed?
- Did anyone else need to get involved in the situation? Who?

5.4   Because we are human, we occasionally ignore routine policies in an attempt to get our work done, especially when we are rushed. Describe the last time you were in this situation.

- What circumstances led to the event?
- In what way did your behavior differ from that required by routine policy?
- What did you do that ignored routine policy?
- How did your behavior affect the patient or your co-workers?
- How did those affected react to the situation?
- What comments did your supervisor make?

♦ How many times would you say this type of situation occurs in a 6-month period?

5.5 In a large hospital, following hospital policy is important. Can you think of a time when you followed a hospital policy with which you didn't agree 100 percent?

♦ What was the hospital policy?
♦ What aspect of the policy did you disagree with?
♦ What was the outcome of following the policy in this
♦ situation?
♦ How often does this type of situation arise for you?
♦ What steps did you take to have the policy changed?

5.6 Tell me about a hospital policy that you had some role in changing.

♦ What was the hospital policy?
♦ How did you become involved in the situation?
♦ What steps did you take in getting the policy changed?
♦ What was the outcome of the situation?
♦ How often do you get involved in such situations over the period of a year?

0.3 Switching focus again, I would like to ask you a few questions with regard to nurse–patient relationships. What sort of rapport do you usually try to develop with patients assigned to your care?

4.2 We are all aware that patients can be very trying at times and often demand services that go beyond our duties. Can you tell me about a time when a patient asked you to do something beyond the call of duty?

♦ What was the request?
♦ How did you react to the request?
♦ What steps did you take in an effort to fulfill the request?
♦ How did the situation turn out?
♦ What was the patient's reaction to the outcome?
♦ How often do these situations occur within a 6-month period?
♦ What comments did your supervisor make about the way you handled the situation?

4.3 Tell me about the nicest compliment you received from a patient in your care.

- ◆ What did you do for the patient that prompted the compliment?
- ◆ What did the patient say when he or she complimented you?
- ◆ Did the patient tell anyone else?
- ◆ How often did this type of situation come up in the past year?
- ◆ Tell me about another incident. [repeat probes]

4.4 Not all patients are so nice. Some are irritating or rude. Tell me about the most irritating patient you have had to care for.

- ◆ When did this situation take place?
- ◆ What did the patient do that was particularly irritating to you?
- ◆ How did you respond to this patient's rudeness?
- ◆ Was the patient satisfied with the way you handled his or her care?
- ◆ Did the patient say anything to your supervisor? If so, what was said?
- ◆ How often do you have to deal with such patients over a 6-month period?
- ◆ Can you think of another instance?

0.4 I would like to finish up by focusing some questions on your co-worker relationships. What are two strengths that you have in dealing with your co-workers?

1.1 Tell me about a time when you used these strengths to help resolve a serious disagreement between two fellow workers.

- ◆ What was the source of the disagreement?
- ◆ What indicated to you that the disagreement was serious?
- ◆ When did you decide to become involved?
- ◆ What did you say to try to settle the situation?
- ◆ How did your co-workers respond to your arbitration efforts?
- ◆ What was the outcome of your intervention?

1.2   Can you recall the last time you were asked to help out with a patient who was not under your primary care?

- ♦ When did this happen?
- ♦ What was your workload at the time?
- ♦ What were you asked to do?
- ♦ How long would it take?
- ♦ What did you do?
- ♦ How successful was your assistance?
- ♦ How often does this type of situation arise over a 6-month period?

1.3   Because nurses have to work shift work that includes weekends, we all look forward to the weekends we get off. Occasionally, though, someone asks us to give up a weekend as a favor to them. Tell me about the last time this happened to you.

- ♦ Who asked you to give up the weekend?
- ♦ What was the reason you were given?
- ♦ How did you react to the request?
- ♦ What did you do?
- ♦ How often does this type of request get asked of you over the space of a year?

1.4   Tell me about a time when at the end of your shift there were still a lot of tasks undone.

- ♦ What tasks were still to be done?
- ♦ How did the nurse coming on after you react to the situation?
- ♦ What did he or she say?
- ♦ How did you handle the situation?
- ♦ What did you do to reduce the incidence of this type of situation occurring again?

1.5   Tell me about a time when you felt the least effective or were most frustrated in your efforts to deal with a conflict between yourself and a co-worker.

- ♦ What was the situation?
- ♦ What exactly did you say and do?
- ♦ What made this situation difficult for you?
- ♦ What was the outcome of the situation?

- What steps have you taken to improve your skills in this area?
- What are the results of these efforts?

1.6 Can you tell me about the last time you took an unpopular stand among your co-workers?

- Who opposed your position?
- How did you defend your position?
- What was the outcome of this situation?
- How did it affect your future working relationship with those who opposed your position?

♦ Part-Time Lab Worker

♦ BEHAVIOR DIMENSIONS

1. Follows routine instructions and procedures consistently and dependably *versus* is inconsistent, forgetful, or careless on routine procedures.
2. Maintains a high level of output during peak demand periods *versus* works at a normal pace during peak periods.
3. Listens carefully and responds in constructive feedback *versus* pays little attention, continues in old ways, or becomes hostile and resentful.
4. Suggests possible improvements in procedures *versus* shows no concern for improving procedures.
5. Accepts routine or unpleasant tasks *versus* avoids, procrastinates, or complains about unpleasant tasks.
6. Works steadily *versus* wastes time when there is work to be done.

♦ INTERVIEW QUESTIONS

0.1 Tell us a bit about your work experiences so far. Start with your most recent job and work backward.

2.1 Let's focus in on your job at [XXX]. Tell me about the busiest rush period you went through at [XXX].

- ♦ How long did it last?
- ♦ What led up to the heavy demand?
- ♦ Is there a particularly heavy day that sticks out in your mind? Can you describe that day for me?

- When did you get in?
- How long did you stay?
- Did your boss say something to you about your work that day? What was said?
- Were there other rush periods at [XXX]? [repeat probes]

4.1 When did you feel most satisfied about something you accomplished at work?

- Describe for me what you actually did.
- Whose idea was this?
- Who helped you on this project?
- Did your boss or co-workers say anything to you about it? What did they say?
- What was the outcome of all this?
- Was there another time that made you feel this way about work? [repeat probes]

1.1 I would like to shift gears a bit now. I know that when mixing chemicals or performing other routine tasks, sooner or later everyone makes a goof. I know I have. I would like you to tell me about the most recent goof you made.

- What actually happened?
- What led up to the mistake?
- What was the outcome?
- Has this kind of mistake ever happened to you before? About how often?
- Did you take any specific steps to remedy the causes of the error?
- What were they?

3.1 Moving on to a different topic, one way we all learn is from feedback from our boss. I would like you to think of the last time your boss took you aside to say something about your performance.

- What was actually said?
- What led up to this incident?
- What did you say in response?
- What did you do about it?
- Had the boss brought up this topic before?
- What did you learn from what the boss said?

3.2 Sometimes, just like everyone else, the boss is wrong. I would like to hear about the time you were most frustrated with something your boss said or told you to do. You were frustrated because you knew you were right.

- ◆ What did the boss say?
- ◆ What was the background to it?
- ◆ What did you say in response?
- ◆ How was it resolved?
- ◆ Has this type of situation come up again? How often?

5.1 All jobs have some unpleasant tasks that are boring or physically uncomfortable. Can you recall the most unpleasant task you were asked to do at work?

- ◆ Who asked you to do this task?
- ◆ What was the task?
- ◆ What was your response when you were asked?
- ◆ How often were you asked to do this task?
- ◆ Was your response always the same?
- ◆ [If different] What was another way you responded?
- ◆ Who among your peers did this task most often? Why?

1.2 Sometimes, the best way to learn is from your mistakes. Can you recall the mistake you made that you learned the most from?

- ◆ What was the mistake?
- ◆ What led to it?
- ◆ What did you learn from the mistake?
- ◆ How did you handle the situation when it came up again?

6.1 There are times on all jobs when things get slack and some-one is not standing right there to tell you what to do. Tell me about the most recent time this happened to you.

- ◆ What did you do?
- ◆ How often have you done that?
- ◆ Did your boss say anything to you about your behavior?
- ◆ What was said?
- ◆ Have you ever handled it differently?

◆ Personnel Officer

◆ BEHAVIOR DIMENSIONS

1. Works steadily and diligently, manages time and prepares for periods of hectic activity *versus* wastes time, does not plan ahead or schedule work according to hectic and slow times.
2. Checks work thoroughly for errors and completeness *versus* makes mistakes.
3. Aids and acts on employees' behalf *versus* neglects employee needs and concerns.
4. Takes *versus* avoids responsibility for tasks from start to finish.
5. Communicates clearly, attentively, and politely to coworkers and employees, handles delicate situations with sensitivity, contributes to a positive work environment *versus* is inattentive, rude, or impatient with peers, is insensitive, and causes resentment and dissension in the workplace.
6. Takes initiative to suggest new programs and solutions *versus* relies on past practice or ideas from others.
7. Maintains a clean, orderly *versus* a disorganized, messy work area.

◆ INTERVIEW QUESTIONS

Recent Work Experience

0.1 I would like to begin by having you describe and explain your tasks and responsibilities in your last position.

1.1 Some days it seems that everyone has a problem they need solved or a question they need answered. Tell me about a time

178

when you had people waiting to see you because your appointment calendar was overbooked.

- ♦ What were the circumstances that led to your being overbooked?
- ♦ How did you handle the situation?
- ♦ What were the reactions of the people waiting to see you?
- ♦ What was your response to them?
- ♦ How satisfied was each individual with the time you spent with him or her and the way you resolved his or her problems?
- ♦ What steps did you take to reduce the occurrence of this type of situation in the future?

1.2 Tell me about the busiest time you experienced recently.

- ♦ When did this happen?
- ♦ What did you do to prepare yourself for the onslaught?
- ♦ How did you know what to expect?
- ♦ How did your preparations pay off during the rush?
- ♦ Did your supervisor ever mention anything about your ability to handle these busy periods?
- ♦ What did he or she say?

1.3 Fortunately, we also experience times that are relatively slack. Tell me about a situation in which you had extra time on your hands.

- ♦ How slack was it compared to your normal workday?
- ♦ What did you do to keep busy during this time?
- ♦ What were your co-workers doing during this period?
- ♦ Did you ask for other assignments?
- ♦ What were these assignments?
- ♦ Tell me about another instance.

1.4 Describe a time when you implemented a procedure to help make your job run more smoothly.

- ♦ What was the procedure?
- ♦ How did you go about organizing it?
- ♦ What was the reaction of your co-workers to this new procedure?

♦ How did it make the running of your job smoother?
♦ How did it affect the jobs of others in your department?

Related Work Habits

0.2   Now I would like to find out a bit about your success in catching and correcting errors. What do you do that helps you pick out errors?

2.1   Tell me about a time when you saved the company money by detecting an error.
   ♦ When did this happen?
   ♦ How did you discover the mistake?
   ♦ What was the error?
   ♦ Who was responsible?
   ♦ What did you do to correct the error?
   ♦ What steps did you take to avoid such mistakes in the future?
   ♦ How could this error have been avoided?

2.2   Can you tell me about a time when you made a mistake in calculating accounts for your company savings plan?
   ♦ What was the magnitude of the error?
   ♦ How was the mistake brought to your attention?
   ♦ How did you correct the error?
   ♦ What was the response of the employee whose account was incorrect?
   ♦ How did you explain the discrepancy to the employee?
   ♦ How did you guard against making such mistakes in the future?
   ♦ How often do such mistakes occur over the space of a year?

2.3   Sometimes, when we are pressed for time, we neglect to check our work to make sure that it is complete as well as correct. Tell me about a time when you were in this situation.
   ♦ What were the circumstances that caused you to neglect this task?
   ♦ What was the effect of this incident?

+ How do you normally go about checking your work for completeness?
+ How did you handle any problems that arose from this incident?
+ What did you do the next time this situation arose?

0.3 An important aspect of the Personnel Officer's job is to aid the employees in understanding policies, benefits, and so forth, and sometimes to act on their behalf. What skills do you possess that help you do this?

3.1 Describe a time when you used these skills on behalf of an employee to overturn a decision that was not made in his or her favor.

+ What was the decision?
+ Who made it?
+ What made you decide to get involved?
+ How did you intervene in the situation?
+ What was the outcome?
+ How were your efforts perceived by the employee?
+ What did he or she say to you?
+ How many times do you become involved in such situations over the period of a year?

3.2 Tell me about a time when you aided an employee in understanding a difficult policy.

+ What was the policy?
+ How did you know that the employee was having trouble understanding?
+ What did you do or say that helped?
+ How did you know that you had been successful in your attempt?
+ What was it about the policy that was difficult?
+ What steps did you take to change the policy so that it would be easier for others to understand?

3.3 Sometimes, we are asked to make exceptions to the rules. Can you recall a time when an employee approached you for a withdrawal from the savings plan after the deadline had passed?

+ What reason did the employee give for missing the deadline?

♦ What did you do?
♦ How did the employee react?
♦ What was the final outcome?
♦ How did this situation differ from others of a similar nature?
♦ How frequent are such requests in a 6-month period?

3.4 Can you recall the last time you were rushed but took the time to answer an employee's questions regarding material readily available in the company manual?

♦ What did the employee want to know?
♦ How did you respond to the request?
♦ How long did it take you to complete the task?
♦ How did it affect your other work?
♦ How often do these types of situations arise within a 6-month period?

3.5 Tell me about the last time you handled a housing loan request for an employee.

♦ What steps did you take in handling the loan?
♦ How did the way you handled this loan differ from the way you usually handle loans?
♦ How long did it take?
♦ What was the employee's response to the way you handled the loan?

0.4 I would now like to focus more on your work habits. In general, briefly describe how you normally go about accomplishing an assigned task.

4.1 Describe for me the last time you were asked to prepare a presentation on short notice and were given very sketchy details as to required content.

♦ What was the presentation?
♦ How did you gather the necessary information to prepare?
♦ What steps did you go through in organizing the task?
♦ Whom did you get to help you with the task?
♦ How did you work around the time constraint?
♦ What sort of feedback did you receive from those who attended the presentation? From your supervisor?

♦ How would you have organized the presentation if you had had more time?

4.2 Can you recall a time when you had to leave a portion of unfinished work in the hands of someone else?

♦ What were the circumstances that led to the situation?
♦ How did the other employee react to the extra work?
♦ What type of instructions did you have to supply to have the task completed?
♦ What did you do to monitor the progress of the other employee?
♦ What do you normally do to keep track of the tasks you delegate?
♦ What comments, if any, did your supervisor make regarding the way the task was accomplished?

6.1 Tell me about the last time you undertook a project that demanded a lot of initiative.

♦ What type of project was it?
♦ How did you become involved in the project?
♦ Why was initiative called for?
♦ What steps did you go through in accomplishing the project?
♦ What obstacles did you encounter, and how did you overcome them?
♦ What was the outcome?

7.1 In this type of position, there is often a large amount of paperwork and many files. Tell me about a time when you were able to put your hands on what you needed immediately because of your system for organizing files.

♦ What were the circumstances leading up to the situation?
♦ What information did you need?
♦ How were you able to get it so quickly?
♦ How did this affect the outcome?
♦ How would the outcome have been different if you had not been able to get the information quickly?
♦ What comments did your supervisor make about the situation and the way you handled it?

7.2 Tell me about a time when you were unable to locate certain papers that were important for a major decision.

- What was the decision?
- How did you go about locating the papers?
- Who else was involved in the search?
- How was the decision finally made?
- What steps did you take to avoid this type of situation in the future?

Communication Skills

0.5 Human resource personnel are continually communicating with people in both good and bad situations. What do you feel is your most effective method of communication? Why?

5.1 Tell me about the last time you had a really good idea and had to persuade your supervisor to accept it.

- What was your idea?
- How did you present your idea to your supervisor?
- What did he or she find difficult to accept about your idea?
- What made the situation especially difficult for you?
- What was the outcome?

5.2 At times, we have to deal with very fragile emotional situations. Tell me about the last time you had to visit the widow of a deceased employee.

- What was the purpose of your visit?
- How did you feel about the visit?
- What did you do or say to help put the widow at ease?
- How did the widow react to you?
- How did this situation differ from the way you normally handle such matters?
- What was the outcome of the visit?

5.3 Can you recall the last time an applicant insisted he or she was the best candidate for a position?

- What was the position?
- What did you say to the applicant?
- How did the applicant react to the rejection?
- What was the outcome of the situation?

5.4 Describe a time an employee requested some confidential information from you.

- Who was the person requesting the information?
- What reason did he or she give for wanting the information?
- What did you say to the person?
- What was the response?
- How was the situation eventually handled?
- How did you handle this situation differently from your normal way?
- What comments, if any, did your supervisor make about the situation?
- How has the outcome affected your relationship with the employee who asked for the information?

5.5 Working effectively with your co-workers is obviously important. Tell me about a time when you used your social strengths to help your co-workers through a difficult time.

- What were the circumstances leading up to the difficulty?
- What steps did you take to improve the situation?
- What was the result of your efforts?
- How was your relationship with your co-workers affected?
- How often have you helped out in this manner in the past year?

5.6 When a group of people work closely together, it is inevitable that conflict will arise. Tell me about the most serious disagreement you have had with a co-worker.

- When did this happen?
- What led to the disagreement?
- How did you attempt to solve the problem?
- What was your co-worker's reaction?
- How was the situation resolved?
- What is your relationship with that person today?
- How often over a period of 6 months did you find yourself in this type of situation?

◆ Probation Officer

◆ BEHAVIOR DIMENSIONS

1. Demonstrates practical knowledge and understanding of rules, regulations, and policies *versus* is uninformed and makes mistakes.
2. Gathers all information relevant to a case in an accurate, thorough, and efficient manner, organizes, interprets, and synthesizes this information to develop appropriate recommendations *versus* makes hurried recommendations based on sketchy or incomplete information.
3. Manages time effectively so that all elements of the caseload get fair attention *versus* wastes time or spends inordinate amounts of time on one case.
4. Writes reports that are clear and complete and require minimal editing and explanation, goes beyond job requirements *versus* fails to follow up on information important to the report, does not check for errors, avoids responsibilities.
5. Develops professional, patient, considerate client contact *versus* is abrasive and intimidating toward clients.
6. Contributes to pleasant, cooperative relations with staff *versus* argues, bickers, causes resentment and dissension.

◆ INTERVIEW QUESTIONS

Recent Work Experience

0.1 Let's begin by having you fill me in on your duties and responsibilities on your most recent job related to our opening.

1.1   In any position related to government agencies, there are many rules, regulations, and policies that need to be understood. Tell me about a time when your knowledge and understanding helped you work through a difficult case.

- ◆ What were the particular circumstances of the case?
- ◆ What rules, regulations, or policies did you find helpful in dealing with the case?
- ◆ How were they helpful?
- ◆ What was the outcome of the situation?
- ◆ What feedback did you receive from your client regarding the way you handled the case?
- ◆ What comments did your supervisor make?

1.2   Now I would like you to tell me about a time when you didn't adhere to the proper rules, regulations, or policies and the results were a bit sticky.

- ◆ What led to the situation?
- ◆ What steps did you take in working through the situation?
- ◆ What reasons did you have for handling the situation the way you did?
- ◆ What was the outcome?
- ◆ How were those involved in the situation affected?
- ◆ How would you handle this kind of situation if it came up again?
- ◆ What were your supervisor's comments?
- ◆ How often does this type of situation occur over a 6-month period?

1.3   Can you tell me about a time when a colleague recognized that you had done the appropriate thing in an ambiguous situation?

- ◆ What was the situation?
- ◆ What was it about the situation that made it ambiguous?
- ◆ How did you handle the situation?
- ◆ What was the outcome?
- ◆ How did your co-worker bring his or her feelings to your attention?
- ◆ How would you handle the situation differently if it came up again?

Related Work Habits

0.2   One of the most important aspects of dealing with any case is making sure that we have all the necessary information. What strengths do you possess in gathering and organizing information?

2.1   Tell me about the time you felt you were most resourceful in gathering information on a particular client's case.
- What was the situation?
- Describe the step-by-step process you went through in obtaining the information.
- Who else did you consult in gathering the information?
- How did you decide that you had gathered all the information relevant to the case?
- What effect did your thoroughness have on the outcome of the case?
- How did the way you gathered the information in this instance differ from the way you normally do it?
- What sort of feedback did you get from your supervisor?

2.2   Sometimes, we have to make recommendations when we don't have all the relevant data. Can you recall the most frustrating time when this happened to you?
- What led to the situation?
- What information were you missing?
- How did the missing information affect your recommendations?
- What options did you consider?
- What was your final recommendation?
- What would your recommendation have been if you had had all the relevant information?
- How did your client react to your recommendation?
- How often do you find yourself in this type of situation over the space of a year?

2.3   When you are assigned a difficult case, organization is important. Can you think of a time when you organized your work effectively, helping you get it done on time?
- What was the case?
- Who assigned it to you?

♦ What steps did you take to organize the case?
♦ How did this organization help you get the case done?
♦ Was the case completed on schedule?
♦ What comments, if any, did you receive on your organization?
♦ How did this method of organization differ from the way you normally organize a case?

0.3 Heavy caseloads are the norm in our profession rather than the exception. Briefly describe for me your personal system for ensuring that each case gets "equal time."

3.1 Tell me about the toughest deadline you've faced when some overtime work was required.

♦ How big a push did you make as the deadline approached?
♦ What made meeting the deadline tough?
♦ What changes did you make in your daily routine to meet this deadline?
♦ How close did you come to meeting the deadline?
♦ How did you feel after you had completed the task?

3.2 One of the more enjoyable aspects of any job is vacation time. Tell me about how you managed to take your most recent vacation.

♦ When did this happen?
♦ What arrangements did you make to ensure that your caseload was covered?
♦ What problems did you have in arranging this coverage?
♦ How did your co-workers react to taking on your cases?
♦ How well were the cases handled in your absence?
♦ What things were left undone on your return?
♦ Tell me about the biggest headache you encountered because of a vacation.

3.3 Now let's turn the tables. Tell me about a time when you were asked to handle a co-worker's caseload while he or she went on vacation.

♦ What was your reaction to the extra caseload?
♦ How did you manage to deal with all of the cases?
♦ How was your regular caseload affected?

- What comments did your clients have about the way you handled their cases during this time?
- What did you learn from this experience?

3.4 Tell me about a time when you requested extra work.

- What work did you request?
- What were the circumstances that led you to ask for more work?
- What was the reaction of your co-workers to your request?
- How often do you ask for extra work over a period of 6 months?
- What effect did this additional responsibility have on your other work?
- What was the outcome of taking on the additional work?

0.4 This next set of questions deals with your ability to write presentencing reports. What skills do you feel you possess in this area?

4.1 Can you think of a specific time when you realized you had made an error on your report that seriously affected your client's case?

- What was the error?
- How was it brought to your attention?
- What did you do to correct the error?
- How was the client's case affected?
- What steps did you take to ensure that this type of error did not get past you in the future?
- What comments did your supervisor make about the error and the way you corrected it?

4.2 At times, it seems as if there aren't enough hours in the day to get everything done. Tell me about the last time you had a day like this and were not able to spend as much time in preparing a client's report as you would have liked.

- What were the circumstances that led to the situation?
- What were some of the things you would have liked to spend more time on?
- How did your preparation of the report in this manner affect the client's case?

♦ How did it change your relationship with your client?
♦ How often do you find yourself rushing through the preparation of a report?

4.3 Tell me about a time when you went beyond job requirements in handling a client's case.

♦ What were the circumstances of the case?
♦ What did you do that was beyond job requirements?
♦ How did you assess that extra effort was needed?
♦ What was your client's reaction?
♦ What was the outcome of your added effort?
♦ What did your supervisor say about the situation?
♦ How often in a 6-month period do you go beyond job requirements?

4.4 We all like to be recognized for work we perform well. Can you tell me about a time you were complimented on a report you had prepared?

♦ Who gave you the compliment?
♦ What did that person say?
♦ What was it about your report that led to the compliment?
♦ How many compliments did you receive last year on your skill in preparing reports?
♦ Tell me about the one that gives you the greatest sense of accomplishment. [repeat probes]

Client Interpersonal Skills

0.5 The people we are most concerned with are our clients. What communication strengths do you have that make you suited for this type of work?

5.1 We all have our own little success stories. Tell me about the most satisfying contact you had with a client when you felt you had really accomplished something.

♦ What did you do for the client?
♦ What exactly did you say to the client?
♦ What was his or her response to you?
♦ What was it about the client's response that made you feel that you had helped?

♦ How often does this type of situation occur over a 6-month period?

5.2 Sometimes, an angry client can get on a person's nerves. Tell me about a time you got mad at your client.

♦ What led to the situation?
♦ What was it that triggered your anger?
♦ What did you say to the client?
♦ What was the outcome?
♦ How did this situation affect your future relationship with the client?
♦ What comments did your supervisor make with regard to the way you handled the situation?
♦ How often did this kind of situation occur over a 6-month period?

5.3 Tell me about the most favorable comment you received from a client.

♦ What did the client say?
♦ What led to this event?
♦ What impact did this event have on your future behavior?
♦ How often did you receive comments like this?
♦ Tell me about another one. [repeat probes]

5.4 Because of the nature of our work, we are sometimes placed in the situation of having to discipline our clients. Tell me about a time when you were in this situation.

♦ What did the client do that warranted disciplinary measures?
♦ What steps did you take in disciplining the client?
♦ How did the client react?
♦ How was your relationship with the client affected?
♦ What would you do differently if you had it to do over again?
♦ What was the outcome?
♦ How often do you have to take disciplinary action with your clients over the space of a year?

Co-Worker Interpersonal Skills

0.6 I would like to finish up by focusing some questions on your working relationships. In general, how do you get along with your fellow workers?

6.1 Can you think of a specific incident when you did something for a co-worker without being asked?

- ♦ When did this happen?
- ♦ What were your reasons for taking this action?
- ♦ How did your co-worker react?
- ♦ What did he or she say?
- ♦ How did this fit in with your other responsibilities?
- ♦ Did your supervisor make any comments? If so, what did he or she say?
- ♦ How often do you help out fellow workers without being asked in a 6-month period?

6.2 It is impossible to get along with everyone all the time. Tell me about the most heated disagreement you experienced at work in the past year.

- ♦ When did the disagreement take place?
- ♦ Who was involved?
- ♦ What led to the disagreement?
- ♦ What contributed to the intensity of the disagreement?
- ♦ How was the disagreement ended?
- ♦ What was the outcome?
- ♦ What is your relationship with that person today?
- ♦ How often did this type of situation come up in the past year?

6.3 Fortunately, all the disagreements we get involved with are not our own. Can you recall a time when you used your social strengths to help resolve a disagreement between two fellow workers?

- ♦ What was the source of the disagreement?
- ♦ How did you know that it was serious?
- ♦ When did you become involved?
- ♦ What steps did you take to calm things down?
- ♦ How did the workers respond to your intervention?
- ♦ What was the outcome of your efforts?

6.4 At one time or another, we are all asked to help out with something when we just don't have the time. Tell me about the last time you were unable to accept additional work.

- ♦ When did this happen?
- ♦ Who asked you to help?

♦ What were you asked to do?
♦ What were your reasons for not accepting the task?
♦ How did the person asking for help respond?
♦ How often did this situation arise in the past year?

6.5   Tell me about a time when you were placed in charge of your unit while your supervisor was away.

♦ What reason did your supervisor give for choosing you?
♦ How did your colleagues feel about your being chosen?
♦ What problems arose during this period?
♦ How was the situation stressful for you?
♦ What did you do to handle the situation?
♦ What comments did your supervisor make about the situation?

♦ Regional Sales Representative

♦ BEHAVIOR DIMENSIONS

1. Enthusiastically develops new client contacts *versus* avoids new client contacts.
2. Presents a positive, balanced view of products *versus* exaggerates product or service qualities to get a sale.
3. Organizes tasks to get the most done *versus* lacks organization.
4. Patiently explains difficult concepts *versus* becomes irritated or rushed when customers fail to grasp the point.
5. Follows through quickly on questions and requests *versus* makes promises but lets things slide.

♦ INTERVIEW QUESTIONS

Sales Experience

0.1 What are some of your qualities that make you suited to sales?

1.1 We all know that establishing new client contacts is an important part of any sales position. Think back to the time you were most successful in establishing new client contacts. Tell me what you did that led to those contacts.

- ♦ When did this occur?
- ♦ How many new clients did you drum up at that time?
- ♦ How many was your average during that period?
- ♦ What did you do at that time that was especially useful?
- ♦ How many hours a week did you spend last month on new client contacts?

1.2   Can you recall the most difficult new client contact you ever made? What happened?

  ◆   What made this contact particularly difficult?
  ◆   How did you approach the difficulty?
  ◆   What was the potential customer's response?
  ◆   What did you learn that was helpful for future calls?
  ◆   Tell me what happened the first time you tried to use what you learned.
  ◆   About what percentage of new client contacts were like this one?

2.1   Sometimes you meet a customer who will agree to everything but actually signing the contract. Tell me about the most difficult time you faced in closing the customer.

  ◆   How did you get the customer to take the product?
  ◆   Did that customer ever take repeat orders?
  ◆   How did you decide on the particular tactic you used?
  ◆   How often have you used this approach in the past 6 months?

2.2   Occasionally, to close a tough sale, we have all had to "stretch the truth" a bit. Tell me about the most recent time this situation came up for you. [If applicant responds "Never"] Perhaps "stretching the truth" is a bit severe. I meant to ask you for the most recent time when you painted a rosy picture to obtain a sale. When was the last time that came up?

  ◆   What did you say that helped get the sale?
  ◆   How did that take liberties with the objective facts?
  ◆   When was the next time this type of situation came up?
  ◆   Has the "rosy picture" ever come back to haunt you later?
  ◆   What happened?

4.1   Another situation faced by sales reps is explaining a difficult concept to a customer who is not technically "up to speed." Think of the time you were most successful in getting a complex concept across.

  ◆   What was the concept you were trying to get across?
  ◆   How did you go about making it understandable?
  ◆   How did you know that you had gotten the idea across?

- Did the customer compliment you or make any comments? What?
- How often did this type of situation come up in the past 6 months?

4.2 Tell me about the most frustrating time you faced in trying to get a difficult concept across.

- When did this occur?
- What was particularly frustrating about this incident?
- How did you tackle the obstacles here?
- What were the short- and long-term outcomes?
- How often did this type of situation come up in the past year?

5.1 Sometimes, we are asked a question that we don't have an answer for at the time. Tell me about the last time this happened to you.

- What was the question?
- How did you handle getting back to this person?
- How long did it take you to find and report the answer?
- Have you ever handled this situation differently?
- [If yes] How did you handle it then?
- Did you ever receive any comments on your answers? What?

General Work Experience

0.2 Moving on to questions of a more general nature, what are your employment plans over the next 5 years?

3.1 Think of the most recent major project you were assigned on the job.

- When did this take place?
- Who assigned the project?
- What was the project assignment?
- Were any deadlines set to complete the project?
- How did you organize your effort on this project?
- Who worked closely with you on this project?
- Did you complete the project on time?

- ♦ What was the long-term success of the project?
- ♦ How did you know the project was a success?
- ♦ What comments did you hear about your work on the project?

3.2 From time to time, we all find ourselves a bit behind on some task. Tell me about the time when you fell furthest behind your list of things to do.

- ♦ What led to your not being able to keep up?
- ♦ How did you try to correct the situation?
- ♦ What was the outcome of your efforts to catch up?
- ♦ How often has this type of situation come up in the past year?

3.3 Tell me about the most recent time when you volunteered to put in overtime or work on your own time to finish a work-related task.

- ♦ What task were you trying to finish?
- ♦ Why was the extra effort needed?
- ♦ Did fellow workers do the same in this situation?
- ♦ What was the outcome of your additional effort?
- ♦ How often has this come up in the past year?

3.4 Many jobs have busy and slack periods. Tell me about the quietest period you experienced in the past year.

- ♦ What led to the drop in activity?
- ♦ What did you do on the quietest day you can remember?
- ♦ What were the other workers doing that day?
- ♦ What comments did you get about your effort?
- ♦ How often did this type of situation come up in the past year?

♦ Secretary/Office Clerk

♦ BEHAVIOR DIMENSIONS

1. Works steadily and productively on tasks *versus* wastes time.
2. Keeps a neat and orderly *versus* a messy work area.
3. Is courteous, considerate, and accommodating toward members of the public *versus* is rude and uncooperative.
4. Develops and maintains positive working relationships with peers *versus* is selfish, argumentative, and uncooperative toward peers.
5. Plans ahead, turns in well-designed work, organizes tasks logically *versus* works carelessly, rushes through tasks without thinking ahead, resulting in work having to be done over.
6. Checks carefully for mistakes, even on routine tasks *versus* skims over finished work, missing mistakes.

♦ INTERVIEW QUESTIONS

Recent Work Experience

0.1 I would like to get started by having you tell me about your duties and responsibilities in your most recent job.

5.1 Everyone has his or her own system for getting things done. Tell me about the way you prepared your working papers for the last project you were involved with.

♦ What were the steps you went through in processing them?

199

- How long did it take?
- What sort of checks did you use in each step?
- Did you ever receive any comments on your method of handling this task?
- What were those comments?

5.2 Tell me about a time when you were able to provide important information to someone immediately because of the way you organized your files.

- What information was required?
- Who was making the request?
- How were you able to provide the information so fast?
- Did your supervisor comment on your efficiency?
- What did he or she say?
- How often did this type of situation arise in the course of a month?

5.3 Sometimes, when we are in a hurry, we tend to rush through a job and don't take as much care in doing it as we ought. As a result, we end up having to do the job all over again. Tell me about the last time this situation happened to you.

- When did this happen?
- What was the task?
- What shortcuts did you take?
- What was the reason you had to do the task all over again?
- How much time did redoing the task cost you?
- How did you handle the task the next time it came up and you were pressed for time?

6.1 Many times clerical staff handle checks for various clients of the company. Tell me about the way you handled the last such check you received.

- What were the steps you went through in processing the check?
- What was your responsibility with regard to the check?
- How did you get the check to the client?
- How long did it take you to process the check?
- Was this your standard procedure in handling checks? If not, how do you normally handle them?

Related Work Habits

0.2   Each office has a pattern of busy and slack times. How do you generally make use of the slack periods?

1.1   Tell me about the most recent slack period you faced.

- When did this happen?
- How slack was it compared to your normal work activity?
- What did you do during this time?
- What were your co-workers doing?
- Did you seek out other assignments during this time?
- Tell me about a time that you did seek out other work.

1.2   During slack periods, some companies allow their employees to utilize some of this time to improve their work skills. Tell me about a time when you took advantage of an opportunity like this.

- When did this happen?
- What activity did you undertake?
- How long did it take?
- How did you schedule this activity into your workday?
- How did this activity contribute to the improvement of your work skills?
- How often did you take advantage of such opportunities?

1.3   Fortunately, not all time is slack time. Tell me about the busiest time you recently experienced on the job.

- When did this happen?
- What sort of preparations did you make in anticipation of this busy time?
- How did you know what to expect?
- How did your preparations pay off?
- Has your supervisor ever commented on your ability to handle these busy periods?
- What did he or she say?

1.4   During busy times, there are invariably deadlines that have to be met. Tell me about the last time you had a deadline to meet.

- What steps did you take to get the task done before the deadline?

◆   Were other people involved in the task?
◆   How close did you come to the deadline?
◆   How often did this type of situation occur within a 6-month period?

1.5 Switching focus a bit, tell me about a time when you really had to push to make it to work on time.

◆   When did this happen?
◆   What led to your being pressed for time?
◆   Did you make it to work on time?
◆   What steps did you take to avoid this situation in the future?
◆   What did you do the next time this situation arose?

1.6 Every now and then, situations arise when we have to leave work for a few hours. Tell me about the most recent day this happened to you.

◆   When did this occur?
◆   What caused you to have to leave?
◆   How did you handle the situation?
◆   When did your supervisor first learn that you were gone?
◆   Did your absence cause any problems at work?
◆   What were they?
◆   How often did this situation occur in the past 6 months?

0.3 Since clerical workers deal with constantly changing information, it is important that reference materials be kept up to date. In general, how do you go about updating such information?

2.1 Many times others require information or materials that we possess but we are not around to give it to them. This could be because we are in a meeting, on vacation, out sick, or just not in our office at that particular moment. Tell me about a time when someone needed something from your office and you were not there to get it for him or her.

◆   What was the needed information?
◆   Was the person able to find it in your office?
◆   How long did it take him or her to find it?
◆   Who else had to be called in to help look?

♦ How did you know that the material had been taken and who had taken it?
♦ How and when did you get the material back?

Public Communication Skills

0.4 Another important aspect of our work is dealing with the public. What strengths do you have in dealing effectively with people?

3.1 Can you remember the most recent time when you went out of your way to help a member of the public?

♦ What led to the event?
♦ What did you do to help the person?
♦ How did the person respond to your assistance?
♦ What were the long-term effects of the incident?
♦ How often did this type of situation occur over a 6-month period?

3.2 We all have days when we feel overburdened and frustrated. On these days, dealing with clients seems to be more of a chore than anything else. Tell me about the most frustrating time when you did not have time to deal with a client.

♦ When did this happen?
♦ What was it about the situation that made it frustrating?
♦ Why couldn't you deal with the situation?
♦ How did you react to the client?
♦ How did the client respond to you?
♦ How was the situation resolved?
♦ What is your relationship with this person today?
♦ How many times have such incidents occurred in the past year?
♦ Did you handle other incidents in the same manner? If not, how did you handle them?

Co-Worker Interpersonal Skills

0.5 I would like to finish up by asking you a couple of questions about your working relationships with your co-workers. In general, what sort of atmosphere constitutes your work environment?

4.1 Sometimes in the course of day-to-day operations, we come across an error or problem that someone else has missed and that could have been important if it had gotten away. Tell me about the most recent time you caught something like that.

- How did you spot the error or problem?
- What did you do to help correct the problem?
- Did your supervisor comment on the situation? What did he or she say?
- What problems were avoided in correcting the error?
- How did you handle the situation the next time it came up?
- How often did you catch important errors like these?

4.2 We all appreciate it when someone helps us out when we are busy. Tell me about the most recent time you helped someone out without being asked.

- Whom did you help out?
- What was the task?
- What led you to offer your assistance?
- How much overtime, if any, was involved?
- Did your supervisor comment on your actions?
- What did he or she say?
- What was the long-range effect of your action?
- How often last year did you help your co-workers in this manner?
- Tell me about another time. [repeat probes]

4.3 Can you think of the last time you were asked to help out on a task that was not directly your responsibility?

- When did this happen?
- What was the task you were asked to do?
- What was your own situation with regard to workload at the time?
- What were you asked to do, and how long did it take?
- Did you have a choice of whether to do it or not?
- Were you able to be of some assistance?
- How often did situations like this happen in the past year?

4.4   In working with others closely day after day, disagreements are bound to arise. Tell me about the most serious disagreement you experienced with a co-worker in the past year.

- ♦   When did the disagreement take place?
- ♦   Who was involved?
- ♦   How did the disagreement get started?
- ♦   How did it end?
- ♦   What was the outcome?
- ♦   How did you handle similar situations when they arose?
- ♦   How often did situations like this occur in the past year?

♦ Small Business Manager

♦ BEHAVIOR DIMENSIONS

1. Demonstrates a thoughtful, informed, and thorough approach to making decisions affecting equipment and operations *versus* makes snap decisions based on incomplete information or hunches.
2. Sets clear performance standards, provides constructive feedback to subordinates, does not overstep personal authority *versus* is ambiguous with regard to expectations, is overly critical of staff, makes statements and promises without proper authority.
3. Projects a helpful and positive professional image of the firm to all outside contacts *versus* bad-mouths the competition.
4. Demonstrates good judgment in job site decisions, directs crew activities responsibly *versus* takes potentially costly short cuts, fails to adhere to standard procedures for work and safety.
5. Concludes profitable negotiations *versus* gives up more than is gained in negotiations.
6. Relies on good recruiting practices *versus* hires friends or relatives, doesn't interview in a thorough, probing manner.
7. Adhers strictly to work quality standards *versus* is unethical and negligent in responsibilities to customers.

♦ INTERVIEW QUESTIONS

Recent Work Experience

0.1 I would like to begin by having you tell me about your duties and responsibilities in your most recent position.

Related Work Habits

1.1 Uncertainty seems to be a permanent fixture in today's business environment. Tell me about the last major decision you made regarding operations where conditions were uncertain.

- What was the decision?
- What was it about the conditions that made the outcome uncertain?
- What factors did you weigh in coming to a decision?
- How did you evaluate the risks involved?
- What was the rationale behind your decision?
- What were the short- and long-term effects of your decision?

1.2 Tell me about the last time your analysis of and recommendations for a particular expansion opportunity paid off.

- How did you become aware of this opportunity?
- What steps did you take in your analysis?
- What were the major factors determining your recommendation?
- What recommendation did you make?
- What was it about the recommendation that proved profitable?

1.3 Describe a time when you played a hunch with regard to equipment purchase and it backfired.

- Why did you choose that particular course of action?
- Whom did you consult concerning the decision?
- What was his or her reaction?
- What was the outcome of your decision?
- What feedback with regard to the outcome did you get from your superior?

0.2 These next questions try to assess your supervisory skills. What are some strengths that you have that make you suited to supervision?

2.1 New employees are often uncertain about what is expected of them on the job. Tell me about the last time you had to explain performance standards to a new hire.

♦ When did this happen?
♦ How did you become aware that the employee was unsure?
♦ How did you make your expectations clear?
♦ What exactly did you say?
♦ How did you know that you had made yourself understood?

2.2 Tell me about a time when you felt it was necessary to talk to an employee about the need for improvement in his or her performance.

♦ How did you become aware of the situation?
♦ How long after becoming aware of it did you take action?
♦ What exactly did you say to the employee?
♦ What was the reply?
♦ What was the outcome?

2.3 Sometimes, we make promises that we cannot keep to motivate people to get things done. Can you recall a time when you were in this situation?

♦ What was the task you needed done?
♦ What did you say that helped get the job done?
♦ How did that take liberties with the objective facts?
♦ What was the outcome?
♦ How did the employee react upon finding out the reality?
♦ What was your superior's reaction to your action?
♦ How did you handle this type of situation the next time it came up?

Customer Relations Skills

0.3 I would now like to focus some questions on your customer relations. What do you think is your greatest strength in this area?

3.1 There are times when a client will sign a contract without fully understanding the conditions. Can you tell me about a time when a conflict arose because of this?

♦ Why did the client sign the contract?
♦ What was the source of the conflict?

- How did you handle the situation?
- What did you say to the client that made the terms of the contract clear?
- What was the outcome?
- How did it affect your future dealings with that client?
- How often does this happen?

3.2 Often we comment on another company's work to our clients. Tell me about the last time you did this.

- What prompted your comments?
- What exactly did you say?
- What was the client's reaction?
- How often do you comment on a competitor's work?

Job Site Experiences

0.4 The next set of questions deals with activities and decisions on the job site. How do you typically oversee work on the job site?

4.1 There are times when we think money can be saved on a job site by finding an alternative way of doing things. Tell me about a time when you tried a shortcut on the job to save money.

- What reasons did you have for trying the shortcut?
- What was the shortcut?
- How did the shortcut affect the cost of the project?
- What was the outcome?
- What comments, if any, did your superior make?
- How often do you attempt shortcuts over the length of a project?

4.2 Tell me about the last time it was so busy at the job site that you were not able to get all the necessary tasks completed.

- What led to the situation?
- What were the factors that contributed to the rush?
- What were the major obstacles that held up the tasks?
- What steps did you take to cope with the situation?
- What was the outcome of those steps?
- How much overtime was necessary?
- What steps did you take to avoid this type of situation in the future?

4.3 Just as there are busy times, there are also slack periods. Tell me about the quietest period you experienced on the job site in the past year.

- What led to the drop in activity?
- What did you do on the quietest day you can remember?
- What did you have the workers doing?
- What comments did you get about your efforts?
- How often did this type of situation come up in the past year?

4.4 Occasionally, working conditions at a job site are not the best. Describe for me the most serious incident that took place because of this.

- Why was the crew working under such conditions?
- What were the conditions?
- What was the incident that occurred?
- What was the cost of the incident in both human and monetary terms?
- Who was responsible for the conditions?
- How could the incident have been avoided?
- How often do incidents like this occur within a 6-month period?
- What action did you take to avoid recurrence of such incidents?

Negotiation Experience

0.5 Finally, I would like to deal with your negotiation skills. What do you consider to be your strength in negotiations?

5.1 Negotiating presents us with a challenge. Tell me about the last time you came out ahead in a negotiation.

- What were the circumstances of the negotiation?
- What did you do to come out ahead?
- How did you convince the other party that the deal was fair?
- How much did you have to tell the other party to get the deal?
- What information were you able to withhold?

♦ How was this deal profitable for you?
♦ How often do you usually come out ahead in such negotiations?

5.2 There are times when we think we got a good deal but it
turns out that, in actuality, we did not. Can you tell me about one
of those times?

♦ What was the deal that you thought you were getting?
♦ How did the other party convince you that it was a good
deal?
♦ What was the deal that you actually ended up with?
♦ What was your reaction to this reality?
♦ Why was it not a good deal for you?
♦ What did you learn from that experience?
♦ How were you able to avoid getting taken the next time
you were in a similar situation?
♦ How many times did this happen to you in the past
year?

6.1 Every business has to hire people. Tell me about the last
time you were in need of several employees in a hurry.

♦ How did you generate your pool of applicants?
♦ What steps did you go through in the selection process?
♦ What did you base your selection decisions on?
♦ How did this differ from your normal practice of recruit-
ing and selecting individuals?
♦ How often have you hired people this way in the past
year?

7.1 Occasionally, customers are dissatisfied with the service
they receive. Tell me about the most difficult customer whom you
eventually satisfied.

♦ What, in particular, was the customer dissatisfied with?
♦ What did he or she say to you?
♦ How did you respond?
♦ What was difficult about the situation?
♦ What did you do that eventually satisfied the customer?
♦ How were future relations with the customer affected?

◆ Staff Accountant

◆ BEHAVIOR DIMENSIONS

1. Provides clear, organized, complete documentation and working papers *versus* prepares disorganized, confusing written material.
2. Develops professional, patient, considerate client contact *versus* is abrasive and intimidating toward clients.
3. Demonstrates practical knowledge of accounting procedures *versus* makes mistakes.
4. Demonstrates an ability to learn *versus* is unwilling or unable to profit from learning experiences.
5. Seeks appropriate guidance and direction *versus* tries to do the job singlehandedly, resulting in mistakes.
6. Thoroughly covers and ties together account details *versus* fails to follow up or omits important details.
7. Offers effective suggestions for improving client profitability or internal control *versus* makes inappropriate suggestions.
8. Manages time, sets priorities, and works steadily *versus* wastes time, is disorganized.
9. Takes initiative, goes beyond requirements *versus* avoids responsibilities.
10. Contributes to good *versus* poor staff relations.

◆ INTERVIEW QUESTIONS

0.1 I would like to begin by having you outline for me any practical experience you have had on summer jobs or others that is related to the job of staff accountant.

[If the applicant has some experience] I would like to focus the next few questions on those relevant jobs you just described.

[If the applicant has *no* relevant job experience, phrase the questions around class assignments: "senior" or "supervisor" becomes "professor" or "teacher."]

4.1 Let's begin with what you learned from your job experience. Being able to learn quickly on the job is important. Tell me about the time you had to pick up an important skill quickly.

- ♦ What was the skill you had to learn?
- ♦ What led to this situation?
- ♦ What did you do that helped you learn quickly?
- ♦ What was the outcome of this situation?
- ♦ When was the next time you used this skill? Tell me about it.

3.1 Having a firm grasp of practical accounting basics is another definite plus. Tell me about a time when you used your practical skills to best advantage.

- ♦ What led to this situation?
- ♦ Who worked with you on this task?
- ♦ What did your supervisor say about this?
- ♦ What did you do that saved time and effort?
- ♦ How often did this type of event come up?
- ♦ Tell me about another one.

3.2 Sometimes, demands are placed on new accountants that stretch their current knowledge. There are always times when we wish we knew more than we do. Tell me about the time you were most frustrated with your knowledge of accounting at the time. (Tell me about the time you most needed to know more.)

- ♦ What did you need to know?
- ♦ How did you try to find it out?
- ♦ How long was it before the problem was solved?
- ♦ What did your senior say about this event?
- ♦ What did you do to avoid this problem in the future?
- ♦ When was the next time this type of situation came up?
- ♦ What did you do then?

4.2 Another time that can be stressful is when you are expected to learn on the run. You are trying to complete program steps and learn at the same time, but the learning is coming more slowly than you would like. Tell me about the most frustrating learning experience you have had.

- What were you trying to learn?
- What were the demands placed on you at the time?
- How long did it take you to actually grasp the material?
- How did the learning problem interfere with other tasks?
- When was the next time this type of problem came up?
- Tell me what happened that time.

1.1 Something else that is important is your working papers. Tell me about the most recent comments your supervisor made to you about written descriptions of your work methods that you had drafted.

- What did the supervisor say?
- How did you react to this assessment?
- What did you do as a consequence?
- Did the supervisor ever have a different kind of comment? What?

[Examination of the applicant's resume for clarity and organization is relevant. Requesting a short biography upon application would also give an opportunity to observe clarity and organization in action.]

5.1 We are also interested in the way you work with your supervisor. Supervisors are there to provide direction and guidance when you need it. Tell me about the time when you made the best use of your supervisor to help you in a tough spot.

- What was the tough spot?
- When did you first know that you needed help?
- How did you approach your supervisor?
- What advice did you receive?
- What did you do to put that advice into practice?
- What was the outcome?
- How often did you get help like this?
- Did this situation come up again? What did you do then?

5.2 I think we all have a story about a time when we charged ahead thinking we knew the best thing to do when we really didn't. Tell me about the time you most regretted not getting advice before going ahead.

- ♦ What did you do that you regretted later?
- ♦ What should you have done in that circumstance?
- ♦ What were the consequences?
- ♦ When was the next time the same situation came up?
- ♦ How did you handle it that time?
- ♦ What steps did you take to avoid this in the future?

6.1 Sometimes you will notice some figures as you go through a procedure that don't make sense. When you look it over, you find a problem that could have been important if it had gotten away. Tell me about the most recent time you caught something like that.

- ♦ What did you do that helped you spot the problem?
- ♦ What steps did you take to correct the problem?
- ♦ Did your supervisor offer any comments on this event? What?
- ♦ What later problems were avoided by your action?
- ♦ When was the next time this kind of situation came up?
- ♦ How did you handle it then?
- ♦ About how often did you catch important errors in the past year?

8.1 When you are assigned a difficult audit task, organization is important. Can you think of a time when you organized your work effectively, helping you to get it done on time?

- ♦ What was the task?
- ♦ Who assigned it?
- ♦ Who was working on it with you?
- ♦ What steps did you take to organize the task?
- ♦ How did the organization help the work get done?
- ♦ Was the task completed on schedule?
- ♦ Did you ever receive a comment on your organization? What?
- ♦ How often did you follow the steps you mentioned when organizing your work?

9.1 Switching topics again, we are interested in how you show initiative to go beyond everyday requirements. Tell me about the best example of that from your experiences.

- What did you do that was beyond the call of duty?
- What led you to take this initiative?
- What was the outcome of your actions?
- Did your senior say anything about your action? What?
- How often in the past year did you show this kind of initiative?
- Tell me about another time. [repeat probes]

8.2   There are always times when things are so busy that you have to keep running all the time and other times when there is little to do. Tell me about the slowest period in your recent experience.

- When did this occur?
- What caused the slowdown?
- What did you do during this period?
- What were your co-workers doing during this time?
- Did your senior comment on your efforts? What was said?
- How often did this kind of slow period come up?
- Did you ever handle it differently? What did you do differently that time?

0.2   I'd like to move away from the purely technical side of the job now and focus some questions on the people aspects of your work experience. What are some strengths you have in dealing effectively with people?

2.1   The people we are most concerned about are our clients. Tell me about a time when you used your people strengths to handle a problem with a client.

- What led to this problem with the client?
- What did you do to help solve the problem?
- How did the client respond?
- What was the long-term outcome of this event?
- How often did this type of event come up in the past year?

2.2   Sometimes, we all run into frustrating customers or clients. Tell me about the most frustrating person you had to deal with recently.

- What specifically did the person do that was frustrating?
- What did you do to resolve the difficulties this created?
- How did the person react to what you said?
- What did you say next?
- Tell me what happened the most recent time you got together with this person.
- How many frustrating people did you run into in the past year?
- Did you ever handle one differently from the way you handled the last one? How so?

7.1 Tell me about a time when you were able to help improve a work procedure by making good suggestions to your supervisor.

- Where did you get the idea for the suggestion?
- What suggestions did you make?
- What help did you get from your supervisor on this suggestion?
- How often were you able to offer this kind of help last year?
- What comments did you receive?

7.2 Sometimes, in spite of the best intentions, something you suggest causes someone else to get irritated. Tell me about the time you most wish you had the chance to rewrite your suggested improvements before they were passed on.

- Who was irritated by your suggestion?
- What specifically irritated that person?
- What were the possible consequences of following the suggestion?
- How was the problem resolved?
- What steps did you take to avoid this problem in the future?
- How often have you received comments on your suggestions?

10.1 Working effectively with your fellow staff accountants is obviously important. Tell me about a time when you used your social strengths to help your co-workers through a difficult time—perhaps an argument you helped settle.

- What was the background to the difficulty?
- What steps did you take to improve the situation?
- What was the result of your efforts?
- How often have you helped out in this way in the past year?
- Did you ever handle it differently? How so?

10.2   Even the best of us—in a way, *especially* the best of us— have disagreements with co-workers from time to time. Tell me about the most serious disagreement you had with a co-worker.

- When did this happen?
- What led to the disagreement?
- How did you first approach solving the disagreement?
- How did the co-worker respond?
- What was the outcome of this disagreement?

◆ Systems Analyst

◆ BEHAVIOR DIMENSIONS

1. Demonstrates efficiency, creativity, and initiative in investigating and implementing solutions for users *versus* inefficient job performance, lacks creativity and initiative.
2. Manages time and projects to meet schedules and budgets *versus* constantly misses deadlines, goes over budget.
3. Discusses plans with users and supervisors, keeps them informed of the progress of activities *versus* does not communicate with users and supervisors and/or ignores instructions from them.
4. Develops pleasant and constructive working relationships with co-workers and users *versus* bickers and withdraws from them.
5. Provides clear, precise documentation *versus* provides documentation that is incomplete and difficult to understand.
6. Demonstrates a willingness to take on additional responsibility or work *versus* avoids challenge, prefers routine work assignments.
7. Demonstrates the ability to follow and constructively criticize company guidelines *versus* is unable to work within the organizational framework.

◆ INTERVIEW QUESTIONS

Recent Work Experience

0.1 I would like to start by having you tell me about your duties and responsibilities at your last job.

Work-Related Habits

1.1 Now I would like you to describe a specific task you found especially difficult to accomplish.

- What was the task?
- How did you happen to be assigned the task?
- What was it about the task that you found especially difficult?
- How did you overcome this difficulty?
- What was the result of your effort?

1.2 We all enjoy being recognized for the good work that we do. Tell me about a time your supervisor complimented you on your work.

- What did your supervisor say?
- What did you do that led to the compliment?
- How many such compliments did you receive in the past year?
- Tell me about the one that gives you the greatest sense of accomplishment. [repeat probes]

1.3 Very few programs are absolutely perfect when first written. Tell me about a time when you had to modify an existing program to enhance its efficiency.

- How did you become aware of its inefficiencies?
- How did you take steps to correct it?
- What were some of the key factors you considered in making the program more efficient?
- What problems did you encounter?
- How did you solve them?
- What was the outcome?
- What were some of the user's comments regarding the outcome?

1.4 Tell me about a time when your research enabled you to find the right solution, not just the obvious one.

- What was the obvious solution?
- What was the right solution?
- How did your research help you arrive at the right solution?

- Who else was involved in the project?
- What were the roles of everyone, including yourself?
- What comments, if any, did you receive on this project?

1.5 Tell me about an incident when a user was dissatisfied with the manner in which you handled his or her request.

- What led to the situation?
- What exactly was the source of the user's dissatisfaction?
- What steps did you take to remedy the situation?
- What was the user's reaction to these steps?
- How many times in the past year did you find yourself in a similar situation?

0.2 I would like to focus now on your ability to meet budgets and schedules. How important was it in your last job to meet budgets and schedules?

2.1 Tell me about the time when you received the most satisfaction from being able to meet the allocated budget and schedule for a project.

- Who was responsible for setting the budget and schedule for the project?
- What steps did you take to bring the project in on time and within budget?
- What was it about the situation that was the most satisfying for you?
- How often do you bring projects in on time and within budget in a 6-month period?

2.2 Unfortunately, not all projects get done in time or under budget. Describe for me the time when you got most seriously delayed in completing a project.

- What caused the delay?
- Who had set the original schedule?
- How reasonable was it?
- What extra efforts did you make to try to meet the deadline?
- How long did the task actually take to complete?
- What comments did your supervisor make?
- What steps did you take to try to avoid this situation in the future?

2.3 Every job has its slack periods. Tell me about the last time you had free time in your last job.

- What caused the drop in assignments?
- What did you do during this period?
- What were your co-workers doing at this time?
- Did you ask for extra work?
- If so, what was it?
- How often did these periods occur in the past year?

2.4 We all have times that we wish we could redo something. Outline the last project you wish you could have redone.

- What parts of the task did you want to redo?
- Why did you want to redo them?
- How were these things done unsatisfactorily to begin with?
- How would you do it differently?
- How many times a year do you wish to have another chance to do something over?

2.5 Tell me about the last time you had to work overtime.

- What circumstances led to the event?
- Why was the overtime necessary?
- How often was overtime needed in a 6-month period?

Interpersonal Skills

0.3 This next section assesses your ability to communicate with users and superiors. Perhaps we could start by having you state a couple of your communications strengths.

3.1 Sometimes, we are not on the same wavelength as the user. Describe to me a time a user wanted something different from what you had in mind.

- What did the user want?
- How did that differ from what you wanted?
- How did you overcome your differences?
- What was the user's reaction to the solution?
- What did he or she say?
- Tell me about another instance. [repeat probes]

3.2 Tell me about an incident when you were able to avoid a major problem because of the close communications you had with the user.

- ♦ What led to the situation?
- ♦ How did you become aware of the potential problem?
- ♦ What was the nature of your communications with the user?
- ♦ How did you keep the user informed of developments on
- ♦ the project?
- ♦ What was the potential problem?
- ♦ How did your contact with the user help avoid the situation?
- ♦ What did you do to avoid the problem?
- ♦ How often were you able to avoid such problems in the past year because of your close association with the user?

3.3 We all need to ask for help every now and then. Tell me about the most difficult assignment for which you needed to ask your supervisor for help.

- ♦ What did you need help with?
- ♦ Why did you need help with it?
- ♦ What was your supervisor's reaction?
- ♦ What did he or she recommend?
- ♦ How was his or her recommendation helpful?
- ♦ What was the outcome of the exchange?
- ♦ How often did you discuss problems with your supervisor in the past year?

3.4 Tell me about the last project you did in which keeping your supervisor informed helped the project progress smoothly.

- ♦ What was the project?
- ♦ How often did you give progress reports?
- ♦ What were some of the key points that you informed your supervisor about?
- ♦ How did these frequent reports aid the smooth completion of the project?
- ♦ How did your supervisor use the information you gave him or her?
- ♦ How was this situation different from the way you normally handle progress reporting?

3.5 We are all guilty at one time or another of assuming that we know the best way of handling a project, regardless of what the user says. Tell me about the most serious problem that arose as a result of your insistence on doing it "your way."

+ What led to the situation?
+ What was the project?
+ Why did you feel that your way was better than the user's?
+ What was the problem that arose?
+ How were you responsible?
+ What did you do to correct the situation?
+ How did you handle it the next time this type of situation occurred?
+ How often did you find yourself in this kind of a situation in the past year?

0.4 I would like to switch from your user relationships to how well you get along with your co-workers. Can you briefly sum up your skills in dealing with fellow employees?

4.1 I'd like you to tell me about a specific time when you used these skills to settle a dispute between two fellow workers.

+ What was the dispute about?
+ When did you first notice it?
+ What were the first steps you took in trying to settle the dispute?
+ What did you say?
+ How did the disputing parties respond to your attempts?
+ How was the dispute eventually settled?
+ How often have you helped out in this type of situation?

4.2 People work at different speeds. Tell me about the most frustrating time you experienced when you had to work with someone whose pace was significantly slower than yours.

+ What were the circumstances of the situation?
+ How was the situation frustrating?
+ How did you attempt to cope with the differences in speed?
+ What did you say to your co-worker to let your feelings be known?

- ◆ What was his or her response to you?
- ◆ What was the outcome of the situation?

4.3 Can you recall a time when you were put in charge of completing a task with a group of people whose personalities clashed intensely and quite frequently?

- ◆ How did you come to be assigned to the project?
- ◆ What measures did you take to ensure minimum conflict?
- ◆ How did you handle the clashes when they did occur?
- ◆ What were your co-workers' reactions to your role in the group?
- ◆ What was the outcome of the group effort?
- ◆ What comments, if any, did your supervisor make about the way you handled the situation?

4.4 Tell me about a time when you helped out a fellow worker without being asked.

- ◆ What led to the situation?
- ◆ What made you decide to offer your assistance?
- ◆ What did you do to help?
- ◆ What was your peer's response to your help?
- ◆ What did he or she say?
- ◆ How often did you do this in the past year?

Documentation and Reporting Experience

0.5 Documentation is an integral part of a programmer's job. How important was documentation on your last job?

5.1 Describe how you documented your last project.

- ◆ How did you document the various sections of the project?
- ◆ How long did it take you?
- ◆ How did this procedure vary from your normal methods of documentation?
- ◆ What comments have you received on your documentation?

5.2   Many times, a problem can be resolved immediately or an error corrected quickly because of careful documentation. Tell me about a time when you were in this type of situation.

- ◆   What was the problem or error?
- ◆   How did your documentation help?
- ◆   How often does this type of situation occur?

5.3   Tell me about the time when you felt the greatest satisfaction from your documentation or from a report that your supervisor commended you on.

- ◆   What did your supervisor say about it?
- ◆   What was it that he or she was especially impressed by?
- ◆   Why did you feel especially satisfied?
- ◆   How did this incident affect the way you handled this task in the future?
- ◆   How many times in the past year did you receive such positive feedback?

5.4   Supervisors aren't always so easy to please. Tell me about an incident when your supervisor was not satisfied with the quality of your report and requested that you rewrite it.

- ◆   What was it about the report that your supervisor was dissatisfied with?
- ◆   What did he or she say to you?
- ◆   What specific changes had to be made?
- ◆   How long did it take you to rewrite?
- ◆   How did you change your method of report writing as a result of this incident?
- ◆   What percentage of your reports had to be rewritten in the past year?

Motivational Experiences

0.6   I would like to switch topics now and focus some questions on how you show initiative to go beyond everyday requirements. How important do you feel it is to demonstrate initiative?

6.1   Tell me about the last time you took on a task that was outside your job description.

- What was the task?
- What led to the incident?
- What made you decide to take on the task?
- How did this task affect your other responsibilities?
- What was the outcome of taking on the task?
- How often in the past year did you show this kind of initiative?

6.2 University courses dealing with our professional interests are becoming more popular. Tell me about a course that you took while working that was job-related.

- What was the course about?
- Why did you choose that particular course?
- How many hours per week did you spend on the course?
- How did this course benefit you at work?
- How often do you enroll in such courses?

6.3 Tell me about the last article you read from which you were able to gain new insights for use on the job.

- What was the article about?
- What was the source of the article?
- What insights did you gain?
- How were they useful to you on the job?
- How was the article brought to your attention?
- How many hours per week do you spend doing such reading?

6.4 Describe the last time you were given additional responsibility and you requested that it be given to someone else.

- What was the extra responsibility?
- What were your reasons for not accepting it?
- What was your supervisor's reaction to your request?
- What did he or she say?
- What was the outcome of this situation?
- How often did you refuse additional assignments in the past year?

0.7 In this final set of questions, I would like to find out how well you work within company guidelines. Briefly explain to me what you feel is the purpose of these guidelines.

7.1 We don't all agree with the guidelines or policies that the company sets down. Describe to me a recent time you followed a divisional guideline or company policy even though you disliked it.

- How did the policy or guideline relate to the task?
- What was it that you disliked?
- How did you make your feelings known to your supervisor?
- What was his or her reaction to your feeling?
- What was the outcome of the situation?
- How was the policy or guideline changed as a result of this incident?

7.2 Tell me about a time when your supervisor provided you with positive feedback because you had followed company procedures well.

- What led to the incident?
- What exactly did your supervisor say?
- How did this affect the way you followed procedures in the future?
- How many times in the past year did your supervisor provide you with such feedback?

7.3 Sometimes, we are asked to participate in policy creation or change. Tell me about an organizational policy you had some role in changing.

- What was the policy?
- How did you become involved in the situation?
- What was it about the policy that you felt needed to be changed?
- What steps did you take to change the policy?
- What was the outcome of the incident?
- How often in the past year did you participate in similar incidents?

♦ *APPENDIX B*

Bottom-Line
Savings ♦

♦ TABLES OF DOLLAR BENEFITS

For readers who would like to determine the approximate dollar benefits of investing in BD interviewing, this appendix provides tables of dollar benefits possible *per hire, per year of tenure.* The numbers in the tables were generated according to a utility formula that has been proved algebraically (Schmidt, Hunter, McKenzie, and Muldrow, 1979). Research evidence supports the methods used to set the control parameters. There are four tables. The following discussion explains how to decide which table applies to your situation and how to use the columns and rows of the tables to zero in on your specific program benefit.

Deciding Which Table Applies to You

The four tables represent four levels of selection accuracy improvement. The improvement you can expect is a function of the methods you are using now. The following rules that direct you to a particular table are ordered from the most traditional to the most advanced current practice. To use the rules, go only as far down the list as your current selection practice implies. The tables are also ordered from the greatest improvement in accuracy to the least. If you are in doubt about which table best fits your situation, choose the table with the lower improvement potential. Be conservative, but be realistic.

1. If an initial screen on the basis of resumes is followed by
    unstructured interviews and reference checks, choose
    Table B.1.
2. If employment interviews are conducted from a standard
    pattern developed on the basis of a review of job require-
    ments, and if most applicants are asked roughly the
    same questions, choose Table B.2.
3. If hiring decisions are made on the basis of interview
    scores the applicants receive *following* a review of inter-
    view notes, or if the applicants' scholastic grades are a
    major factor in deciding whom to hire, choose Table B.3.
4. If the results of ability tests are combined with scores
    from a structured interview, choose Table B.4.

Deciding Which Row Applies to You

Deciding on the proper row to use in a table is easiest of all.
Each row represents one of nine different selection ratios. The
selection ratio is the number of job openings divided by the
number of applicants. When this ratio approaches 1.0, it means
that the organization has little chance to select, because it has to
hire almost any minimally qualified applicant just to fill its
positions. The smaller the selection ratio, the greater the opportunity to choose. A ratio of .2 implies that about five applicants
are reviewed for each opening. Considering the recent economic
recession, there may be more qualified applicants available than
in the past, so try to get the most recent data for deciding how
many applicants will show up for openings over the next two or
three years.

Deciding Which Column Applies to You

Deciding on the proper column is a bit trickier and requires
a judgment call on your part. The columns represent nine different levels of the spread of performance in dollars on an annual
basis (SD_y). Determine an SD_y for your job. Hunter and Schmidt
(1983) have noted that most SD_ys for jobs they have analyzed fall
between 40 and 60 percent of annual salary. If you can't decide
on an SD_y for the job you are analyzing, use 40 percent of annual
salary as a conservative estimate. Then, to pick the proper col-

Table B.1
Dollar Benefits per Hire per Year of Tenure, for a Validity Difference of .4

SR	SD_y								
	2,000	4,000	6,000	8,000	10,000	15,000	20,000	30,000	50,000
.900	160	320	480	640	800	1,200	1,600	2,400	4,000
.750	336	672	1,008	1,344	1,680	2,520	3,360	5,040	8,400
.500	640	1,280	1,920	2,560	3,200	4,800	6,400	9,600	16,000
.400	776	1,552	2,328	3,104	3,880	5,820	7,760	11,640	19,400
.300	928	1,856	2,784	3,712	4,640	6,960	9,280	13,920	23,200
.200	1,120	2,240	3,360	4,480	5,600	8,400	11,200	16,800	28,000
.100	1,400	2,800	4,200	5,600	7,000	10,500	14,000	21,000	35,000
.050	1,648	3,296	4,944	6,592	8,240	12,360	16,480	24,720	41,200
.010	2,136	4,272	6,408	8,544	10,680	16,020	21,360	32,040	53,400

SR = selection ratio (openings/number of applicants); SD_y = spread of performance in dollars on an annual basis.

Table B.2
Dollar Benefits per Hire per Year of Tenure, for a Validity Difference of .3

					SD_y				
SR	2,000	4,000	6,000	8,000	10,000	15,000	20,000	30,000	50,000
.900	120	240	360	480	600	900	1,200	1,800	3,000
.750	252	504	756	1,008	1,260	1,890	2,520	3,780	6,300
.500	480	960	1,440	1,920	2,400	3,600	4,800	7,200	12,000
.400	582	1,164	1,746	2,328	2,910	4,365	5,820	8,730	14,550
.300	696	1,392	2,088	2,784	3,480	5,220	6,960	10,440	17,400
.200	840	1,680	2,520	3,360	4,200	6,300	8,400	12,600	21,000
.100	1,050	2,100	3,150	4,200	5,250	7,875	10,500	15,750	26,250
.050	1,236	2,472	3,708	4,944	6,180	9,270	12,360	18,540	30,900
.010	1,602	3,204	4,806	6,408	8,010	12,015	16,020	24,030	40,050

SR = selection ratio (openings/number of applicants); SD_y = spread of performance in dollars on an annual basis.

Table B.3
Dollar Benefits per Hire per Year of Tenure, for a Validity Difference of .2

SR	SD_y								
	2,000	4,000	6,000	8,000	10,000	15,000	20,000	30,000	50,000
.900	80	160	240	320	400	600	800	1,200	2,000
.750	168	336	504	672	840	1,260	1,680	2,520	4,200
.500	320	640	960	1,280	1,600	2,400	3,200	4,800	8,000
.400	388	776	1,164	1,552	1,940	2,910	3,880	5,820	9,700
.300	464	928	1,392	1,856	2,320	3,480	4,640	6,960	11,600
.200	560	1,120	1,680	2,240	2,800	4,200	5,600	8,400	14,000
.100	700	1,400	2,100	2,800	3,500	5,250	7,000	10,500	17,500
.050	824	1,648	2,472	3,296	4,120	6,180	8,240	12,360	20,600
.010	1,068	2,136	3,204	4,272	5,340	8,010	10,680	16,020	26,700

SR = selection ratio (openings/number of applicants); SD_y = spread of performance in dollars on an annual basis.

Table B.4
Dollar Benefits per Hire per Year of Tenure, for a Validity Difference of .1

					SD_y				
SR	2,000	4,000	6,000	8,000	10,000	15,000	20,000	30,000	50,000
.900	40	80	120	160	200	300	400	600	1,000
.750	84	168	252	336	420	630	840	1,260	2,100
.500	160	320	480	640	800	1,200	1,600	2,400	4,000
.400	194	388	582	776	970	1,455	1,940	2,910	4,850
.300	232	464	696	928	1,160	1,740	2,320	3,480	5,800
.200	280	560	840	1,120	1,400	2,100	2,800	4,200	7,000
.100	350	700	1,050	1,400	1,750	2,625	3,500	5,250	8,750
.050	412	824	1,236	1,648	2,060	3,090	4,120	6,180	10,300
.010	534	1,068	1,602	2,136	2,670	4,005	5,340	8,010	13,350

SR = selection ratio (openings/number of applicants); SD_y = spread of performance in dollars on an annual basis.

umn, choose the column closest to the value of the SD_y you have chosen. Now you are ready to begin calculating your potential savings.

Using the Tabled Number to
Calculate Savings

In checking out the savings possible through better interviewing, we suggest that you make your projection on a 3-year basis. That is, first figure out roughly how many openings you will have over the next 3 years for the job in question. In doing a cost-benefit study, a key decision concerns the benefit period. Given that money is spent to improve selection accuracy, it would be unrealistic to write off all the startup costs of training and pattern development against the savings from only the first year of hiring. Obviously, you could never drill for oil under such a rigorous accounting system. Similarly, for selection investments, the dollar benefits of improved accuracy may well be maintained for years. We chose a period of 3 years because projecting the number of openings and the number of applicants becomes very risky beyond that period. For the next step, estimate the number of applicants you will consider, on the average, for each opening. Then, once you have chosen a table, column, and row, you will have a dollar figure for the benefit per hire, per year of tenure of the hires who stay in the position. The total benefit is the tabled dollar figure multiplied by the number of hires and their average tenure. Your savings will equal that benefit minus costs.

Costs include, first, the cost of developing interview patterns and training staff in behavior description interviewing. This cost should be no more than $4,000 to $6,000 for the first job family, and the cost goes down as more jobs are added. Costs also include the extra time it takes to complete and score a behavior description interview. Our experience suggests that it takes about 1.5 times as long to interview and score an applicant from behavior description interviews as from traditional unstructured interviews. To determine your current costs, multiply the average time you now take on an interview by what your organization pays for that time. To figure the increased interview costs, multiply half of your current costs by the number of interviews you anticipate over the next 3 years. Finally, to get total costs, add the $4,000 to $6,000 in developmental costs to these costs of interviewing.

◆ CALCULATING COSTS, BENEFITS, AND SAVINGS

This section gets down to the nitty-gritty of costing selection program outcomes, and it may not be everyone's cup of tea. The discussion here assumes a basic knowledge of algebra and some experience in using statistics. Don't feel bad if you grind to a halt in the middle of the next page. This is "high-tech" material for the selection expert. However, you do not need to be an expert in utility application to be an effective interviewer. You can use the tables of dollar benefits without understanding the mathematics of it all, just as you use an electronic digital watch without knowing how 15,000 transistors tell time.

Adding up the costs of selection programs—from the money spent to start the flow of applicants down to the last dollar spent to inform the rejected applicants of their fate—has never been the problem. Cost accountants who are capable of the task abound. The problem has been coming up with reasonable dollar estimates for the benefits. Traditionally, selection program benefits have been captured in such terms as "acquiring the cream of the crop" or "maintaining a tradition of outstanding personnel." Many annual reports assert: "Our human resources are our greatest asset." Yet throughout human resource programs, practitioners have been unable and even unwilling to put a dollar value on that asset. Broad maxims sound fine, but hard dollars alone get the serious attention that leads to sound levels of investment.

The basic mathematical relationships among selection program attributes and the dollar benefits they produce have been available since the 1950s (Cronbach and Gleser, 1966). Recently, the careful work of Frank Schmidt and John Hunter and their colleagues has resurrected the selection utility equation and demonstrated its use (Schmidt et al., 1979).

One of the formulas from the Schmidt et al. (1979) paper is applicable to the task of projecting bottom-line savings through investing in behavior description interviewing. In symbolic form, the formula is as follows:

$$U=[(t) \ (N_s) \ (r_2-r_1) \ (SD_y) \ (O/p)]-[(N_s(c_2-c_1)/p]$$

where U = the savings in dollars due to improved interviewing,

t = the tenure of those selected in years,

N_s = the number of openings,

r_2-r_1 = the improvement in selection accuracy, measured as the population correlation for applicants between performance on the predictor (interview, tests) and performance on the job,

SD_y = the annual standard deviation of performance in dollars,

O/p = the bell-curve advantage that comes from selecting from more than one applicant,

p = the selection ratio (openings divided by number of applicants), and

c_2-c_1 = the difference in the dollar costs of selection per applicant under the traditional versus the behavior method.

In words, the bracketed part of the formula to the left of the minus sign calculates the elusive benefit side of the cost-benefit comparison. (The cost side is on the right.) The dollar benefit over random selection is the product of the average tenure in years, times the number of openings, times the improvement in selection accuracy, times the standard deviation of performance in dollars, times the bell-curve advantage derived from the excess of applicants over openings. The costs include advertising and "headhunting" fees, salaries paid to interviewers, and general overhead charges. The one-time costs of developing interview patterns and training managers to use them must also be considered.

The formula is not all that complex. It can be derived algebraically from the simple regression of an applicant's predicted dollar value to the organization to actual value. We haven't specified exactly how the bell-curve selection advantage (O/p) term is obtained, but Schmidt et al. (1979), Landy, Farr, and Jacobs (1982), and Janz (1982) give all the mechanical details.

There is not much debate on these terms. Why, then, has it taken from the 1950s all the way to the 1980s for the formula to be used?

The answer is that—as with any formula—the numbers that come out of this formula are only as good as the numbers that go in. The formula is not the problem—the problem is the estimates of two of the five components of the benefit side. The average tenure, number of openings, and even the bell-curve advantage of multiple applicants per opening are numbers people can accept. The stumbling blocks have been the estimates of selection decision accuracy and the standard deviation of performance in dollars (SD_y). Of the two, the SD_y has been the greater headache.

Recent research, however, has found the cure for both ills. We will take the accuracy question first. It seemed that selection decision accuracy could not be pinned down for a particular selection method. Accuracy varied from method to method and from job to job. Therefore, it seemed that it was necessary to conduct a validity study at each plant for each prediction method and for each job. The accuracy estimates produced by such validation studies varied widely from place to place. In addition to the infamous instability of selection accuracies, only companies with many openings could afford to conduct validation studies of any kind. For most organizations, such a process was simply beyond reach and so became irrelevant. Fortunately, the villain has turned out to be the measure of selection accuracy itself— the correlation coefficient—*not* the tests, interviews, or jobs being studied.

The correlation coefficient between predicted and actual job performance, the measure of selection accuracy, requires a very large number of hires in a validation study to provide a stable picture of the actual selection accuracy. Validation studies conducted on as few as 30 to 50 hires just don't have the statistical power to tie down population selection accuracy. Making things worse are the problems of unreliable criteria of job performance and restriction of range. Unreliable criteria often result from measurement of job performance according to a single supervisor's report on a few vague scales. Restriction of range results when a selection study does not hire randomly from the applicants and then check out actual job performance against predictions made on the basis of tests or interviews. Many selection studies aren't so thorough. Instead, they check out test or interview performance against performance ratings for currently employed workers. This may take much less time, but it is less comprehensive because the ranks of current workers do not include the full range of winners, losers, and average people who show up as applicants. Both restriction of range and criteria unreliability act to *lower* the index of selection accuracy.

Fortunately, new research procedures have overcome these problems. Schmidt and Hunter (1981) have reported how the technique of meta-analysis puts the lie to several old myths about selection testing. This new technique allows researchers to add together the results of many separate studies. Whereas any one of the studies, taken alone, would be too small to generate stable measures of selection accuracy, taken together, a clear picture emerges. Also, Schmidt and Hunter (1981) included statistical corrections for restriction of range and criteria unreliability, and they found that ability tests are valid and useful predictors of performance on all jobs. They combined data from hundreds of small studies, in effect creating one big study of more than 370,000 people. Validities ranged from the .20s for simple jobs to the high .60s for cognitively demanding jobs. Although only a few studies have reported findings for patterned behavioral interviews, they have consistently shown validities in the .40 to .55 range (see Chapter 2). Combining ability tests with behavioral interviews may boost selection accuracy even further, although we don't know this yet. However, we now have a much better handle on selection accuracy than ever before.

The second problem that held back savings analysis was just as serious. The problem was estimating the annual spread of performance in dollars, stated in standard deviation units (SD_y). Managers agreed that it was possible to measure dollar performance for sales jobs and even for some manufacturing jobs for which measures of quantity and quality were gathered regularly. At the same time, managers and researchers alike (Cronbach and Gleser, 1966) were uncomfortable with existing ways of tallying up a person's total annual dollar return to the organization for technical, professional, service, or managerial jobs. Schmidt et al. (1979) suggested a simple, direct estimation method for obtaining SD_y. They had supervisors judge the total annual dollar return in goods and services for an average performer. Then they had the supervisors judge the total return for performers in the 85th percentile. Finally, the supervisors were asked to estimate the dollar performance of workers in the 15th percentile.

Using bell-curve principles, Schmidt et al. (1979) then calculated SD_y as the mean of the 85th–50th and 50th–15th percentile comparisons. Any one supervisor might be way off base, but over a large number of supervisors, errors of over- and underestimation would wash out.

Such direct estimates are quick, but they are often considered "dirty" as well. Managers have used such phrases as "blue-sky estimates" and "guesstimation" to describe them. Schmidt and his colleagues have offered no compelling reasons why the direct estimate method should work. Fortunately, however, two recent studies suggest that various methods for estimating SD_y, including the simple, direct estimates method, are often in close agreement. Bobko, Karren, and Parkington (1983) had 13 supervisors of insurance sales people make estimates of the total annual sales of sales staff in the 50th, 85th, and 15th percentiles. They compared the SD_y calculated on the basis of the direct estimates with the actual SD_y from sales records. The two values were \$54,000 and \$51,000, respectively. Bobko et al. (1983) suggested that having the supervisors zero in on a common estimate for average performers first, before going on to make independent estimates for performers in the 85th and 15th percentiles, might improve the direct method. Janz and Etherington (1983) had 42 supervisors of staff accountants in public accounting firms complete a direct and a detailed behavioral estimate of SD_y. The behavioral estimate was based on judgments of 34 specific job outcomes. The outcomes were market-valued, and the annual impact was costed out. The SD_y based on the rated behavior of 168 staff accountants was \$8,700, and the SD_y based on the simple, direct estimate was \$8,975. When different methods of getting at the same number—the SD_y in this case—agree so closely, it raises our confidence that the methods are zeroing in on the real thing.

Thus, the two brakes on the use of savings analysis have been released. Recent research on determining the accuracy of different selection program methods has allowed us to get a fix on the accuracies of existing techniques. Also, recent research on estimating the standard deviation of performance in dollars gives confidence that even simple techniques provide an accurate estimate of the number needed in the equation. However, now that we can prove the equation using basic algebra and we can demonstrate the quality of the numbers that go into the equation, we are left with a loaded choice. We can still choose *not* to believe the savings that result—but it would be hard to pretend that we are being logical about it. Some people will just never accept the importance of having the best people for the job. After seeing the figures, however, the baldness of such an emotional reaction is evident.

♦ A VERBAL SAVINGS REPORT

The final section of this appendix is an exercise that tries to make the advantages of behavior description interviewing clear in a different way. The exercise is intended for line or human resource managers. Taking the executives or line managers who are responsible for selection program decisions through the exercise before the bottom-line figures are costed out may help generate their interest in seeing what those figures are. It may also add credibility and meaning to the numbers once they are added up.

Better Interviewing Benefits: An Exercise

This exercise helps bring the dollar impacts of better selection down to earth for your particular situation. The exercise will work best if you think of all your employees as working at one particular type of job (e.g., clerical, district sales, staff accountant, systems analyst). It also helps a great deal to have at least ten employees working in the given position. Follow each of the following steps, one at a time, in sequence.

1. Think of your very best employee. To anchor that person in your mind, fill in a first name or nickname here: _____.
    What does *this employee do* that leads you to assign the top rating?

2. Now think of an employee who is closest to average. That is, this employee is half-way down the scale; about an equal number of employees are better and an equal number worse than this employee. To anchor this person in your mind, fill in a first name or nickname here: _____. What does *this employee do* differently from your top employee?

3. Now think of your bottom performer. Every organization has one. To anchor that person in your mind, fill in a first name or nickname here:

_____. What does *this employee do* to be the "worst" in your opinion?

4. Finally, think of the employee who is half-way between your top person and the person you rated as closest to average. To anchor this person in your mind, fill in a first name or nickname here: _____.

5. If you continue to hire using traditional methods, you can expect about half of your new hires to fit between your best and your average performers. About half will fit between the average and the poorest performers. That makes sense on the basis of the odds.

6. If you are using standard interviews now, and if you will consider from five to ten applicants for each opening, adopting behavior description interviewing will lead to the following:
   a. About half of your new hires will fall between the employee named in point 4 (the 75 percent performer) and your best performer.
   b. Average performance will move up from the employee named in point 2 to the employee named in point 4.
   c. Instead of half the new hires falling below the employee named in point 2, only 25 percent will.

7. As a last step, think of all the things the employees in this group could accomplish that they can't do now if three-quarters of the new hires fitted in above your previously average performer and if fully 50 percent of your new hires fell between your 75 percent performer and your best performer. What might some actual improvements be?

♦ REFERENCES

Bobko, P., Karren, R., and Parkington, J.J. 1983. Estimation of standard deviations in utility analysis: An empirical test. *Journal of Applied Psychology, 68,* 170–176.

Cronbach, L.J., and Gleser, G.C. 1966. *Psychological tests and personnel decisions.* Urbana: University of Illinois Press.

Hunter, J.E., and Schmidt, F.L. 1983. Quantifying the effects of psychological interventions on employee job performance and work force productivity. *American Psychologist, 38,* 473–478.

Janz, J.T. 1982. Personnel decisions: Costs, benefits, and opportunities for the energy industry. *Journal of Canadian Petroleum Technology, 21,* 80–84.

Janz, J.T., and Etherington, L.D. 1983. Comparing methods for assessing the standard deviation of performance in dollars. Proceedings of the Annual Conference of the Administrative Sciences Association of Canada, Vol. 4.

Landy, F.J., Farr, J.L., and Jacobs, R.R. 1982. Utility concepts in performance measurement. *Organizational Behavior and Human Performance, 30,* 15-40.

Schmidt, F.L., and Hunter, J.E. 1981. Employment testing: Old theories and new research findings. *American Psychologist, 36,* 1128-1137.

Schmidt, F.L., Hunter, J.E., McKenzie, R.C., and Muldrow, T.W. 1979. Impact of valid selection procedures on workforce productivity. *Journal of Applied Psychology, 64,* 609-626.

Index ◆